THE CURIOUS ONE

"This story touched my heart, inspired me, and made me want to savor every single moment of life. I couldn't be more happy that Chelsea has decided to share her story that until now very few knew. Buckle up and enjoy the journey."

—SHAWN SHEPHEARD, *sugarfreeshawn.com*

"Chelsea's life journey has taken her into places that would be daunting for most of us. Her tenacity and creativity allowed her to turn her extraordinary challenges into a masterful business. She is a guiding force for women everywhere—especially those who need a map. Go where Chelsea leads."

—INDRANI GORADIA, *indranislight.org*

"Her energy, commitment and drive is quite astounding and it's unsurprising she has a big story to tell. A wise woman before her time."

—KAY WHITE, *wayforwardsolutions.com*

"Chelsea is sharp, strategic and dedicated. Read this if you're curious what a new definition of business success could look like."

—LAURA ROEDER, *lkrsocialmedia.com*

"Chelsea is a force of nature. I remember working with her when she was struggling and yet, she always remained positive, upbeat and worked hard regardless of what was going on around her. Chelsea was a rabid learner and always looking for ways to grow personally and professionally. I had no doubt that she would be successful and have been thrilled to watch her grow her own business. She is a superstar and someone I am proud to call a friend."

—DAVE DEE, *davedee.com*

"This is the perfect book on how we emerge from suffering and challenge with real, encompassing wisdom and love. Full of personal growth and emotional fulfillment."

—MIKE FLANNERY, *stopunderachievingnow.com*

"It's rare these days to find someone like Chelsea who actually does what they say when they say it. I had the honor of working with her first hand and was impressed over and over at her drive, commitment, and her ability to not let anything stop her."

—MARC OSTROFSKY, *wordofmouse.com*

"A book of wisdom, compassion, and piercing honesty."
—TAMARA GOLD, *tamaragold.com*

"Chelsea has a no ego, no fear attitude that is essential to entrepreneurism. There are few people that truly understand marketing, and even fewer that have the drive to turn that passion into success. Chelsea exhibits both, and freely offers her wisdom to anyone willing to listen. It's this ironclad resolve, mixed with pure spunk that has me convinced she'll be successful in whatever endeavor she sets her mind to."
—BRIAN JAMBOR, *infusionsoft.com*

"From the first time I met her, I knew that Chelsea was wise beyond her years. It certainly appears that she is successful at just about everything she does. I would read this book and start doing what Chelsea has done."
—DAVE SHERMAN, *infusionsoft.com*

"A powerful story of loss, love and redemption that will stir the souls of it's readers and remind you you're not alone."
—GABRIELLE BERNSTEIN, *gabbyb.tv*

the
CURIOUS
ONE

the
CURIOUS
ONE

from FOOD STAMPS
to CEO

ONE WOMAN'S JOURNEY THROUGH
STRUGGLE, TRAGEDY, SUCCESS & LOVE

CHELSEA BERLER

Published in Birmingham, Alabama, USA by Chelsea Berler.
Printed at Brandt Doubleday, Davenport, Iowa, USA.
thecuriousbook.com

ISBN-10: 1-60087-006-6
ISBN-13: 978-1-60087-006-4

AUTHOR CONTACT
Chelsea Berler
5184 Caldwell Mill Rd, Suite 204-102
Birmingham, AL 35244
800-780-8388
hello@thecuriousbook.com

Book cover design and layout by Jill Anderson @ solamaragency.com
Author photograph by Siddiqi Ray @ auray.com

First Edition

This book is dedicated to my husband, Mark.

I had no idea how hard putting the way I feel about you into words—and then showing those words to the world—would be.

Because really, there are no words that can possibly express what having you in my life has meant to me. At least not words that are big enough, or powerful enough, to express what I want to say.

But I'll try anyway...

Thank you for loving me. All of me.

And for showing me how incredible life can really be.

You're my light.

You're my inspiration to strive to be a better person every day.

You're an incredible, incredible human being.

Thank you for being my anchor.

For keeping me grounded, yet always knowing when I needed you to keep me afloat.

I love you.

Always and All ways.

CONTENTS

FOREWORD

 *I'll have what she's having.*

—WHEN HARRY MET SALLY

Let's face it, a lot of shitty things can happen in life. Whether it be running out of money and going hungry again this month, an awful argument with someone you love, an honest-to-God tragedy, or just road rage because a truck rolled over on the road, making you late for work... every single moment of our lives, something is definitely happening!

Some of the things that have happened in Chelsea's life are nothing short of astonishing. It's almost as if she lived through these ups and downs, slaying dragons on the way, and finding the pot of gold at the end of the rainbow, just so you and I could read about them, because they are a little bit crazy and very inspirational. This is the kind of stuff people make movies about.

Except it's not made up.

It's real.

How does someone not only survive, but thrive through so much adversity? *The Curious One* pulls the curtain back on exactly that. As you read this, you might be going through a difficult patch, or, maybe you're someone who has a hard time finding the positive in life, in general, and wishes you could change that. You might also be interested in how someone took her small-town roots and built a life of contribution on a global scale.

In these pages, you will get a front row seat to all that and what makes Chelsea tick.

The Curious One is a feel-good book, that's for sure. But it also has a very practical message. You see, I was one of her first clients, and 5 years later, am still one of her very happiest—and now proud to be a colleague and a friend for life.

Solamar Agency, the full service boutique implementation firm she built, is the embodiment of Chelsea's other superpower: helping people—especially entrepreneurs with big dreams—get amazing things done. The stories you read will also show you not only how to dream a big dream, but how to make the dreams real.

Turn the page and begin your journey to becoming more curious—adventurous, faithful and smart—in your own life. Let each of the stories sink in. And may this be the moment YOU become the person people think of when they quote from the movie *When Harry Met Sally*.

Chelsea Berler? With all the joie de vivre she radiates? There are just some people I feel proud to represent being human.

"I'll have what she's having!"

Andrea Lee
CEO, Wealthy Thought Leader

Life is an opportunity, benefit from it.

Life is beauty, admire it.

Life is a dream, realize it.

Life is a challenge, meet it.

Life is a duty, complete it.

Life is a game, play it.

Life is a promise, fulfill it.

Life is sorrow, overcome it.

Life is a song, sing it.

Life is a struggle, accept it.

Life is a tragedy, confront it.

Life is an adventure, dare it.

Life is luck, make it.

Life is too precious, do not destroy it.

Life is life, fight for it.

—MOTHER TERESA

PART I
GROWING UP

CHAPTER 1

INTRODUCTION

I'm not telling you it is going to be easy,
I'm telling you it's going to be worth it.

—ART WILLIAMS

The Big Moment came when I was doing my taxes. I know, figuring out what number you have to write on that check to Uncle Sam is not usually the most exciting time in a person's life. But for me, it was a huge Moment—one that had major significance.

It was about two years ago. I was 27 years old, and I'd been running my own business, Solamar Agency, for about five years.

One of my very dear friends was our financial guy (and still is). He'd been with us the whole time. Since the beginning. But when we started out, we were really, really small. So while he was taking care of all the financial stuff for me, I never really thought much about it.

In fact, because I was so focused on serving my clients and my team and putting one foot in front of the other and just doing my work, I never really paid all that much attention to the reports he sent me at the end of every month, year after year. You know, those Profit and Loss statements with the numbers on it that explained just how much money we were making every month?

But then I got that one, life-changing year-end report. And it said my company made about $500,000 that year.

Me. At 27. Just made half a million dollars.

Wait a second—how did this happen?

I sat there and kind of stared at the number on the report, like it would suddenly make perfect sense to me if I looked at it long and hard enough.

Or maybe the "5" would suddenly turn into a "2"... or some other, more reasonable, number that made more sense to me.

But that didn't happen. It wasn't going to happen. Because as I sat there staring at the paper, it started to sink in.

Maybe it did make sense. Maybe it really was possible.

I thought back over the years I'd been running my business. Basically, what I'd been doing was working my tail off. I was going through a lot—I'd gotten my second divorce (Yes, at 24—more on that later...) and the way I dealt with it was just by working, working, working.

That was pretty much my coping mechanism for any sort of problem that might come up in my life. I worked my way through it. It gave me something positive to do that distracted me from whatever was making me feel crappy at the time.

Not like I was super-ambitious or some major *planner.* I wasn't necessarily thinking about my goals, or where the business was going, or even *if* the business was going. For me, the simple fact that I was getting some money at the end of the month after making payroll and paying all the other bills was like, "This is great."

Eventually, I got over the divorce and met an incredible man. But I kept on working. It was the way I defined myself.

And looking at that report, and at the giant, massive, very grown-up number on it, I realized what had been sneaking up on me for years.

All that work had paid off. I really did have a real business.

This was a real thing.

Maybe the fact that, right around the same time, we had opened up our first physical office could have provided a clue. Some sort of, "Hey, progress is being made here" kind of message. But I never really equated opening the office with "success." It was more about my lifestyle. I had been a hermit for such a long time, sitting at my computer in my house working, that basically, I just wanted to get out of the house. I wanted to have a place to go to work, and people to talk to when I got there. I'd been hiring people virtually for years, but I had started hiring people locally. And I needed a place to put those people...

I never expected it all to add up to half a million dollars. But suddenly, I realized that I did it. It happened.

And it was a pretty amazing moment.

I was flooded with all these feelings.

I finally felt like I had made something of myself.

Like I was part of something bigger than me.

Like I wanted to tell everyone to screw off.

I felt *real*.

It was the last place people (especially those people I wanted to tell to screw off) expected to find me.

And that's maybe the biggest reason the whole 500k thing freaked me out. I grew up knowing, or thinking I knew, a pretty depressing fact. That NOT everything is possible.

Pretty much the opposite of what you're supposed to grow up knowing, right?

I grew up in a very small town in North Dakota, with very little money and even fewer possibilities. Not that there was (or is) anything wrong with the town or the people in it. They made me who I am today. I love North Dakota and I'll be forever grateful for my roots.

But it's just the kind of town where everybody knows everybody, and you get married and you stay there and you have kids and your kids stay there and everybody stays there forever and ever and ever.

I never, ever thought I would see another state, or even get out of my little town.

I had no idea how that would even be possible.

They have this one, very specific life path they teach you in school to help you succeed.

1. You go to high school
2. You go to college—usually an in-state school.
3. You become a teacher, or a doctor, or a lawyer.
4. You come home and work and raise your family there.

It's a perfectly great plan for people who want to be doctors or lawyers or teachers.

But that just didn't feel like me.

Of course, like in every town big and small, there are also the dropouts that don't go to college; they don't even stay in high school. So they don't do anything with themselves except maybe sit at the local bar.

I didn't see myself as one of those people either.

And then there are the people who don't go to college, but just have a bunch of cute babies and stay home and live on a family farm.

That's where I figured I fit in. I always assumed I was going to end up married with kids in my hometown. That's what most people like me did. Or pretty much what all people like me did. How could I think I was going to be any different?

The problem was, deep down inside, I *felt* different.

There was a part of me that was always rebelling against "the way things were." I had these vague dreams of "arriving," although where I was going to arrive, I wasn't quite sure. Or wishing and hoping that I could create something lasting, not that I had any idea what that would be.

I just knew that I wasn't like everybody else.

And in my town, in my world, that wasn't exactly a comforting feeling. I was scared as Hell that I would fail, that I wouldn't have anything to show for myself and wouldn't be able to create anything at all.

But that didn't stop me from having visions of something different. Something bigger.

I just didn't know what it would be.

Now, twenty years or so later, I do. Which, I guess, is why I'm writing this book.

As I write this, two years after that moment with my tax forms, my business is hovering right under the million-dollar mark.

And because I have reached this level of success, before turning 30, suddenly, I'm getting noticed. Suddenly, people look at me and think things like, "Oh, she is smart." Or, "Oh, she does have something going on."

Which makes me laugh—because they didn't always feel that way!

I was the girl that didn't fit the mold. That didn't follow the path. How was I ever supposed to be successful if I didn't conform and do what I was supposed to do?

But here's the more important point—maybe you feel like that too.

Because a lot of people do.

Maybe no one ever told you that there's a bigger world out there, and that you can not only get out in it and see it and be a part of it, but actually add something to it.

I know no one told me. I had to figure that part out on my own.

So I'm here to tell you that you do have options. I was a person who was born into a life where there didn't seem to be a lot of options. But I had them—they just weren't immediately visible.

And you have them too. You really do.

Living a life that fits you and makes you happy, leaving your mark on the world even if you don't exactly know what that mark will be, is possible.

You don't have to do it their way.

You just have to find your way.

People might tell you you're crazy. They might say what you want isn't possible. They may—and this hurts—even tell you they don't believe in you.

It doesn't matter.

As long as you stay curious, and stay thirsty for more, and keep trying new things and reaching for new experiences, anything is possible. I know it is. Not only have I lived it, but I'm still living it today.

Sure, there are times when I think that I could lead an easier life—I could stop running all over the country, hang out with my husband and just have fun and relax. Maybe someday I will. But right now, I want more for myself.

And I also want more for people that haven't had that opportunity to be curious.

Because if all this could happen for a girl from Scranton, North Dakota, it can happen to you too.

Are you curious? Then come with me...

CHAPTER 2

HUMBLE BEGINNINGS

If I find in myself desires which
nothing in this world can satisfy,
the only logical explanation is that
I was made for another world.

– C.S. LEWIS

My journey started in a town you've probably never heard of. I was born in Hazen, North Dakota, the youngest of three girls—my big sister Alicia is five years older than me and my middle sister Jessica is three years older than me (they both ROCK!). I also had a half-brother, my dad's son Sheldon, who stayed with us a lot growing up. I considered him nothing short of a brother—and a big brother at that—he was awesome.

We were a really close family. My mom, Debra, has always been my rock. She's my best friend, my world—

there just aren't enough words to describe what she means to me. All I can say is, without her, I think I'd be in a padded cell!

My dad, Scott, was the one person who thought I could do no wrong (even though, as you will soon see, I could do quite a bit). I was his baby, and he adored me. Alicia was like a second Mom to me, and Jess was like my enforcer—she wasn't afraid of anything and wouldn't let anyone mess with me.

Right after I was born, we all moved back to my dad's home town of Scranton, North Dakota, population somewhere around 300. Which is probably why you've never heard of that town either. We moved there so he could work at the local coal mine and help out on my grandpa's farm.

I remember how in love my parents were back then. Some nights I'd wake up really late and look out the window and see them dancing on the deck. They were so romantic. I loved to watch them, and dreamed that someday, I'd be just as in love. To this day, my mom still tells me stories about my dad and how great a man he was. I'm thankful for the stories and I'm so grateful my mom continues to remind us of him.

Maybe that's why I'm such a hopeless romantic.

But I also learned very young that sometimes, romance just isn't enough.

My dad was awesome—cool and sporty and just the kind of guy a girl would fall head over heels in love with. He was super smart and very funny and I loved hanging out with him. But he had an illness.

He was an alcoholic, and that really stripped him of his promise, his ability, and ultimately his life.

I loved my dad so much. I thought he could do no wrong, the same way he felt about me. Looking back, I think I felt a huge responsibility for him because so many people gave up on him. I wanted him to get better, I wanted him to be back to normal.

I loved him enough for everyone. I wanted to always make sure he was loved.

It was a hard way to grow up, and eventually, it started affecting me in school. When they called my mom and told her that the issues with my dad were making me really sad, I'll never forget what she said to me.

She looked at me and said, "You worry about your little girl problems and your Dad will worry about his big boy problems." But I was still worried. I asked her, "What if no one else loved you but me." I was all about love—I made it my mission to try to make everyone love each other.

But sometimes it just wasn't possible. Sometimes it seemed like everyone was frustrated and mad and angry at my dad.

Because of his disease, he was in and out of treatment centers, and the only way to see him was to get in the van and drive two hours each way to visit him. Those car rides were long, and I was a naughty kid who liked to... let's say experiment with things. And one of those little experiments had been putting coins in those little slots in the seat belts of our van.

I swear, I didn't do it maliciously. It was just so cool that I could slide the coins in there...they fit so perfectly... and then they were gone! The problem was, once they were in, there was no way of getting them out. Not for me, and definitely not for my mom. And we didn't have the kind of money to take our car to the shop and pay some mechanic just to get the coins out of our seat belts.

So, thanks to my curiosity, our seatbelts didn't work. No big deal. Until one time we were driving back from visiting my dad at the treatment center and got pulled over. The cop walked up to our van, saw a bunch of kids bouncing around with no seat belts in sight, and got ready to do his official duty and write my mom a ticket.

And she started crying.

I'll never forget my poor Mom, telling this poor policeman all about the struggles in her life. In our lives. He just said, "Ma'am, have a great day"...and let us go.

That was the really awesome thing about where I grew up. Sometimes, when you least expected it, people were really, really kind.

BORN CURIOUS

Sadly, the Seatbelt incident was just one of the problems I caused when I was little. It wasn't that I wanted to hurt anybody. I was just...curious. I wanted to push the boundaries. I always wanted to know what would happen *if...*

For example, when I was in preschool. You know that game where your teacher shows you a card with a color on it, and you say what the color is, and everyone gets excited about how smart you are because you know what green is?

Well, when my teacher would show me a color and ask what it was, and I'd say, "You know what that color is."

I wasn't much more cooperative with shapes. She'd show me a triangle, and I'd snap back, "You know what that shape is."

Seriously? I was a little kid. She was an adult. Did she really need me to tell her what a triangle was?

Okay, so maybe I was being a little bratty. I, personally, think I was just interested in cause and effect. How would they react if I didn't do what everyone else did? What would happen? It was another "what if" situation.

But the powers that be at the preschool confused curiosity, or even bratty-ness, with there being something seriously wrong with me. They actually had me re-screened to make sure I belonged in preschool, and not some other kind of school, or program.

Or cage.

Another big "what if" moment was when I cut my sisters' hair while they were sleeping. I didn't do it to be mean, I just wanted to see what would happen. And it was awesome—they didn't even wake up.

Unfortunately, the hair did not grow back. And my styling skills were not any better than my color-identifying skills.

The salon had to cut spikes in their hair the next day to cover up the bald spots—and to make sure they didn't look completely ridiculous for school pictures the following week (oops!).

When it came to me and my limitless curiosity, nighttime was definitely prime time. That was when I could sneak around and check stuff out and nobody would know what I was up to.

Sometimes I would wake up in the middle of the night, when everyone else in the house was asleep, and I'd go outside—with no clothes on and in zero degree weather (hello, North Dakota!).

Then I'd walk to my neighbor's house.

Then I'd walk inside (no one locked their doors in my hometown!).

And then, I'd realize I was hungry, so I'd get something to eat out of their fridge!

Of course, my neighbors would wake up and find a little kid rummaging through their fridge and immediately call my parents and say, "Do you know where your daughter is?" My mom would say "Of course, she's sleeping."

Or so she thought...

Needless to say, my parents did not find my adventures all that amusing. They were scared to death that I would hurt myself. They had to lock me in my room at night to keep me from getting out and wandering around.

I would even have to knock on my bedroom door so they would let me out when I had to go pee.

In fact, thanks to my endless desire to explore anything and everything, they were always worried about my safety. And my neighbors joined my preschool teachers in the general consensus that Something was Wrong with Chelsea.

My mom, who was always in my corner, always answered the same way. "She's just curious."

LEAVING HOME

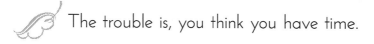 The trouble is, you think you have time.

—BUDDHA

One night, when I was around six, my mom packed up a few things and loaded all of us in the van to go see her sister, my aunt Diana, in Montana.

I didn't realize we were leaving for good.

I was too young to really understand what was going on. All I knew is that I was really sad. And my dad was really sad too, which made me even sadder.

My mom was just a mess. She had to make a really difficult decision and she knew it was time to say goodbye. She tried so hard to make it work (almost 10 years). But my dad was hurting himself while she watched and lived with it, and tried to raise four kids while dealing with it, and she just couldn't keep living that way.

Me? I just remember feeling bad for everyone.

We went to Montana, where my mom grew up, so her sister could help us get back on our feet. Once we arrived at our destination, my dad needed the van—so we were on our own without a car or a place to live—or really anything at all.

We stayed there for about a year and then moved back to North Dakota, to a slightly bigger town called Bowman (1,500 people! The big city!) that's about 13 minutes away from Scranton. We were closer to my dad, which was nice. I got to see him more often.

Until the accident.

I don't really remember the details, only that it was a big accident and we (meaning my dad, my sister—and I) were semi-involved. And after it happened, because of my dad's involvement, my mom was faced with a choice: either tell my dad, "You can never see your kids again," or let us have supervised visits with his parents there. She didn't want us to lose him completely, or him us. So the only way I could see my dad was with my grandparents there at the same time, to make sure all was well.

Unfortunately, bad things were happening when it came to my dad.

His disease was catching up with him, and he got really sick. He couldn't work, so he couldn't pay child support, so my mom wasn't getting any help. Well, except for a check for like $100 from the government that came every month to help her take care of us kids. Which was crazy.

So we lived in low-income housing while my mom worked like three different jobs—working in a nursing home, cleaning other people's houses—and waitressing at a local restaurant.

That's around when I first realized we were poor.

I remember going to the local Jack & Jill grocery store. And my mom was so embarrassed that we were on food stamps (it was a small town where everyone knew everyone) that she asked me to go in instead of her and get some cheese and milk. That moment made an impression on me.

I remember thinking to myself, "I don't ever want to be in this place. I don't want to grow up and not be able to pay for my own food."

The holidays were especially hard. It started in October. Our Halloween costumes were always homemade—and sometimes embarrassing. Plus, we couldn't afford the bags of Halloween candy everyone else gave out, so Mom took the jar where she used to put loose change (tips from waitressing tables!) and handed out a few pennies to each trick-or-treater.

One year, the week before Thanksgiving, a couple from our community appeared at our door bearing a turkey for us, because we were poor.

Which is just another example of how caring the people in our town could be. We do take care of our own in North Dakota.

I also remember my mom showing me how to mix powdered milk to put in my cereal, because milk was so expensive that we couldn't always afford the regular kind. I wanted real milk. And I think that may have been a moment that I realized I was going to work really, really hard to figure out a way that I could help my family.

It's not like we were the only poor people in our town. Nobody there was exactly rich—Oprah and Donald Trump and their friends don't build their mansions in Bowman, North Dakota. But I still felt like we were different. I definitely noticed that the other moms and adults in general treated my mom differently. And I didn't like it.

I felt like I had to grow up fast to protect her and take care of her.

Of course, being poor affected me too. Remember when you were in school how those monthly Scholastic book orders would come in, and all the kids would pick out whatever they wanted, and a few weeks later they'd pass out the books and everyone would get to take them home?

Well, I never got to take any home. Because I never got to order any.

When we went on class trips, I never had any money with me. But my mom did pack me snacks and left me a note in my lunch box. Which, looking back, may be more than some of the kids got.

I definitely had love.

The hardest thing was probably sports. The fees and the uniforms were just too expensive for our family to handle. So our rule was that we could each participate in one thing, because that was all we could afford.

Which made me feel even more different than I already felt.

I was sad that I couldn't participate in things and be on a team and wear a cool uniform like other kids. I was sad that I had to drink powdered milk sometimes, and that we were on food stamps, and that we lived in low-income housing instead of a regular house that we owned, that belonged to us.

But that wasn't my biggest concern, even as a little kid.

My biggest concern was my family.

I constantly worried about my family—mostly my mom. I just wanted her to be okay.

She deserved so much more. But as a girl in elementary school, what could I possibly do to help?

CHAPTER 3

THE BOB FACTOR

Do the best you can until you
know better. Then when you
know better, do better.

—MAYA ANGELOU

Help did come—for all of us. Not from me, but in the
form of a guy named Bob.

Bob was not a new person in our lives. He had been a
friend of my parents for years—I probably met him when I
was really little. As a divorced guy, he had the distinction of
being the only single person in their social circle. My mom
was always trying to fix him up with her girlfriends—she
always said he was a "catch"—although, apparently, she
was not attracted to him.

Little did we all know, she would be the one to catch
him.

When my parents started divorce proceedings, and we
moved to Ekalaka to be closer to my aunt, one convenient

side-effect is that we were now, also, closer to Bob. He was working as a carpenter around the same area. When the divorce was final, my mom invited him to come by our new place from time to time.

I loved him immediately.

I know, I know. I loved everyone. But Bob was special. He was nice to us and took good care of my mom. He even loaned us a car because my mom didn't have one. In fact, it seemed like whatever we needed, Bob was there to do whatever he could and offer help and support—without wanting anything in return.

Almost from the beginning, he was like a kindred spirit. We wanted the same things. Mostly, we wanted to help my mom. We wanted to make her life easier and better. Bob didn't just want to date her, he wanted to be a part of raising us kids.

He wanted a relationship with all of us.

But this was all going on during what was the hardest time for my mom. She had divorced my dad, who she had been passionately in love with, and was dealing with the pain of leaving him when he was sick while trying to figure out how to make ends meet and take care of three kids at the same time.

Add in the fact that we were poor and owned nothing, and you can imagine just how hard it was.

Still, we had moved to Montana because my aunt wanted to help my mom. Now Bob was helping too. So she had two people who were both willing to help her pick up the pieces and get through this incredibly hard time.

Which was nice...

Except for the fact that my aunt and the rest of my mom's family were not exactly Fans of Bob.

It wasn't Bob's fault. He certainly didn't do anything to make them dislike him. I can't imagine him ever doing anything like that—he was (and still is) one of the most decent, caring people I've ever known.

But my mom's family didn't know that.

All they knew was that, just a few months after she divorced my dad, there was suddenly this new guy hanging around my mom. My sad, vulnerable mom. She had already been through so much pain. No one wanted to see her get hurt again.

So Bob had his work cut out for him in winning them over.

He had a hard time in our household too. I was too young to judge him, I was just happy to have any new person around to hang out with—and as you already know, I pretty much loved everybody.

But Alicia was not happy.

And Jessica rebelled a bit too.

After everything our family had been through, everything that happened with our dad and to our mom, Alicia and Jessica both weren't having it. They just wanted to protect Mom...

But the thing they wanted to protect her from, of course, was Bob! The poor guy didn't have a chance.

Alicia and Jessica thought for sure this Bob person was going to hurt her, so they kind of dedicated themselves to making him miserable—because they thought it was the only way to save our mom from more heartbreak.

Luckily, we can all look back on this now and laugh...

When I look back, I see it as a miracle that Bob actually stuck around. Not only were Alicia and Jessica rough with him, not only was my mom still kind of a basket case, but the idea of taking on a family of four in complete free-fall... it's quite a package!

But Bob accepted us all with open arms. Because that's the kind of person he is. He never, ever tried to be our dad or replace him, but he knew we needed a father figure.

And he was definitely that for us.

As amazing as he was, Bob was *not* the kind of person my mom was used to being in love with. He's not an emotional person or one to want to "talk about it." When I first met him, he could barely hug right—he patted.

(Now he's much better.)

After all those moonlight dances on the porch with my dad, Bob's idea of romance was more along the lines of Chinese food and Fudgcicles. He didn't like to spend money—which was actually kind of a good thing, since there was never a lot of money around to spend. But that whole thing about being wined and dined and sent flowers in a box?

That wasn't Bob's style.

Ultimately, I think my mom fell in love with him because he was funny—and that he accepted all of us like a package deal. He wanted to take care of us—and that meant more to Mom than anything.

Personally, even as a little kid, I was really impressed by Bob's work ethic. The man had boundless energy and worked so, so hard to keep everything going. I think watching Bob was the first time I realized that I was going to have to work hard to get what I wanted from life. I will be forever grateful to him for teaching me that.

Once we got settled in Ekalaka, my life resumed as "normal." I already had a new best friend to hang out with. And she was a lot of fun to be with, because she was curious too.

One day, we decided that we really wanted to go the beach. But since there was no beach nearby—and my mom was at work—we decided we'd make our own beach.

In our rental house. On the floor.

The two of us hauled tons of sand into the house for our beach. We worked really, really hard to build it. And when my mom came home from work, she found us kicking back and enjoying it—wearing our swimming suits, making sand castles...in the kitchen.

Needless to say, my mom had no words for what she witnessed.

I'm pretty sure Bob cleaned up the "beach."

LIFE WITH BOB

Bob had been in our lives for a few months when we moved to low income housing in Bowman, North Dakota. Which also happened to be the town where Bob lived.

By this point Mom was working at the nursing home full-time—which meant 12 hour shifts. But no matter how hard she worked, the money still wasn't enough. She struggled to pay the bills and provide the basic necessities of life for her three kids.

So Bob came up with a solution. He invited my mom to bring all of us and move into his house.

And after talking it over, my mom agreed.

At first, it was more like a "shared housing" arrangement than anything romantic. Bob slept on the couch while he and Mom slowly, carefully built their relationship. And we weren't just sharing the house with Bob, but also his sons from his first marriage. Mason, who was a little older, lived with his mom, so we hung out with him during the holidays and also in the summer. But Brady, who was my age, moved in with us full-time.

Brady was a lot like Bob—full of life and bursting with energy—plus he was in my grade at school. So we definitely hit it off. It was kind of like having a twin brother.

Not to mention a partner in crime.

Still, even though Bob had "rescued" us, money was tight. Mom didn't get any child support for us other than that $100 a month from the government. Meanwhile, Bob was paying $350 a month in child support for his kids. Back then, that was a fortune—it basically ate up one of my mom's entire paychecks.

So while you might think our lives would have gotten easier from a financial standpoint when we moved in with Bob, it was just as hard as ever. It was another year before we could get off of food stamps. And later, when we did, buying our own food left us with no extra money to spend.

I remember once we were at the grocery store and my mom was writing a check. I saw in her register that she had a $100 balance. To me, that seemed like a fortune. I said, "Mom, you have a lot of money!" Then she said, "That has to last our family the whole month."

So the money thing didn't get much better. But we weren't alone anymore. We were taken care of in every way without money.

We had everything we needed.

BECOMING A FAMILY

By this time, Bob had won the family over—even my dad. They bumped into each other at a bar, and my dad walked up to Bob, whose immediate response was to reassure him, "I just want you to know that nothing was going on while you were married."

My dad said, "If I was going to pick anyone to be with Deb and the kids, it would have been you."

My mom still cries when she tells this story.

After about a year, Mom and Bob were ready to make it official and got engaged. Even then, Bob still slept on the couch when the kids were there—he didn't want us to think that sleeping with someone before marriage was okay. In the end, Bob and my mom didn't actually share a room for almost two years of dating and living under the same roof—which has to be some kind of world record!

When the big day came, Mom and Bob tied the knot in a church—my grandmother insisted that it wasn't right to get married anywhere else. So we had a ceremony with all the kids there and our immediate family. Of course, since

Bob wasn't exactly Mr. Big Spender, it was a low, low, low budget wedding. So low budget that Mason and Brady added water to the punch to try to make it last longer.

That Christmas—the first Christmas my mom and Bob spent as man and wife—Bob started a tradition that has stayed with our family ever since. He pinned a dollar onto the Christmas tree, so no matter what happened, we would always have money at Christmas.

I don't mean to make it sound like we were all perfect. Of course, there were still some aspects of Bob that we weren't crazy about—especially us kids. And most of those things related to his profound dislike of spending money. We had to abide by some crazy, ridiculous rules, such as:

We weren't allowed to talk on the phone after 8PM.

We had to hang out all of our clothes to dry on a clothesline, because a dryer cost too much.

He even brought us girls outside to watch the meter as he ran a blow dryer, just to "educate us" as to how much money our perfectly smooth and sleek hair was costing the family!

But Bob's tightwad-ish ways had a bright side.

TRAVELS WITH BOB

The entire family worked an extra job—all together—to earn money so we could afford a vacation in the summertime.

It was, and I don't think I'm exaggerating here, THE WORST JOB IN THE WORLD.

The job was cleaning the sales barn of our local town. Yes, we were literally cleaning up cow shit! Plus scrubbing floors and bathrooms after each cattle sale.

Ohmigod, WE HATED THIS JOB! We tried to think of anything and everything to get out of it. But Bob stayed firm.

And when we finally went on those vacations, they were absolutely the best. They made everything worth it.

I still giggle just thinking about those times.

We took our trips in a minivan with a pop up camper. The first trip was to Disneyland in California. Later, we went to the Wisconsin Dells, to Disney World in Florida and even Alaska.

They were seriously the best trips ever.

Of course, we had no money. With our family, that was a given. So when it was time to eat, we made peanut butter and jelly sandwiches out of the trunk of the van. We got all of our food at the grocery store and made it and ate it on the go.

And we never went out for dinner. EVER!

Well...we actually tried it once. We went to a restaurant, sat down and got served water. Bob took one look at the menu and decided the grilled cheese was too expensive.

So we walked out.

We had more fun eating PB&J anyway.

SAYING GOODBYE

Love with all of your heart. You cannot save people. You can only love them.

—CHELSEA BERLER

Unfortunately, while we were establishing our new life with Bob, my dad was losing his battle with alcoholism.

My dad went to rehab several times, but it never seemed to stick. Eventually, it got so bad that the entire family gathered for what I guess was an unofficial intervention.

My mom initially didn't want us kids to go, and today, I understand why. It was one of the saddest things I've ever witnessed—our family sitting around in a circle, telling him how much we loved him and needed him to stop drinking. But my mom and my Uncle Mark made a deal and my mom let us go with him…and I'm glad we went. I think it might have made a difference for a while.

But not forever.

He just kept getting sicker and sicker—he had Hepatitis C, and combined with drinking, that's just a horrible combination. When I would see him, he just looked yellow, because his liver was failing. If I touched him, even lightly, it would indent his skin (I think that's called edema). But I still had no idea how sick he was. I just knew he wasn't feeling well. He was in and out of hospitals all the time, but I didn't know why. All I knew was that he had some troubles with drinking.

The truth was, my dad was also a Curious One—in so many ways. He was so talented in all kinds of different areas, but he couldn't quite get it all together, and it ended up seeming like the world was against him. I think he got to the point where he felt like he didn't have a choice, that he didn't have the life he thought he'd have.

And so he was hard on himself in every way.

I loved him so much. I also felt responsible for him when I felt like so many people were giving up on him. So I spent extra time at my Grandma and Grandpa's house—where he was living—and really just soaked up that time with him. I always felt like he needed a friend, so I tried to be with him all the time.

And I was.

Plus, seeing my dad meant I also got to see my grandparents, who I also adored. We were very close—they'd been (and remain) a huge part of my life. Grandma and Grandpa were the most amazing people, and stayed madly in love for 64 years until I lost my grandma just this last year. They've always been there for me, even though, as committed Christians, they haven't always approved of my choices!

But when it came to love, I could always count on them.

Still, they didn't talk much about what was happening to my dad. I can't imagine what they were going through watching this happen to their son. It must have been extremely painful.

But we lived in a small town. And one thing about small towns is, people talk. One of my friends' moms worked at a hospital, and she knew about my dad, and she happened to tell her daughter, my friend, that my dad was dying. The next day at school, my friend told me.

I was devastated.

The second I saw my mom I told her what I'd heard and asked her if it was true. The first thing she did was call the other mom on the phone. I remember her saying, "How dare you?"

Of course, what they were saying about my dad was true. But Mom wasn't ready to go down that road with me yet. She didn't want me to worry or feel sad. So she sat me down and calmly explained to me that my friend and her mom had no idea what they were talking about.

I don't remember the last time I saw him.

He had gone back to college and was living in Fargo. I called him every night. Then one night—I think it was the 4th of July—I called and he didn't answer. The same thing happened the next night. And the next.

I was starting to worry. This wasn't normal.

Finally I told my mom he hadn't called and I hadn't been able to reach him. She told me not to worry. I told my grandma, and she said the same thing. Everybody said not to worry.

But I was worried. I was incredibly worried, even though no one else seemed to be. He and I talked every night. Something was wrong.

Around the 7th of the month, other people in the family started to worry too. They also started calling, and no one could reach him. No one had any idea where he was.

By the 10th, someone called his neighbor and they looked inside his apartment. He had passed away in his sleep.

He was dead for about a week before anyone found him.

We got the call in the middle of the night. Alicia took my hand and just held it and had me sleep with her. She was in terrible pain too, but she never forgot to look out for me. Eventually, we all ended up in my mom's bed that night. We just laid there holding hands…wide-awake. Quiet.

I was 11 years old.

Later, they did an autopsy that showed he probably died on July 4th—that first night when I couldn't reach him and just felt inside that something was wrong. That's the date they put on his headstone.

The autopsy also said he died of "natural causes." I call bullshit on that one. I don't think what alcohol did to my father's body could possibly be considered "natural."

On July 11th we all gathered at my grandma's. It was her birthday, but we weren't there to eat cake or blow out candles. We were all there together because her son had passed away.

The funeral was in my hometown of Scranton. My dad had to be cremated, because his body sat for so long in that apartment. I remember a little black box sitting at the front of the altar.

I remember Mom walking us in.

And beyond that, to be honest, I don't really remember much of anything. Except just feeling numb. Despite the way he'd looked, despite the rumors going around our town, despite the fact that he'd been in and out of hospitals for years, I just couldn't believe it happened.

I couldn't believe my dad was really gone.

And later, his passing made me feel even more different from everyone else. I remember that I didn't know anyone that didn't have a dad (or that had ever lost a parent), so none of my friends really understood or were able to help me with it. It ended up being just another area of my life where I didn't understand where I fit in…because I felt like, "Now, I'm really different. Everyone has two parents but me. How did my dad die so young? This isn't normal."

Looking back, I know my mom kept a lot from us to keep us as sane and healthy as she could through all of the hard times. She wanted to shield us from the bad parts. And there were a lot of bad parts.

But my mom was not one to dwell on the past. She was always looking toward the future. Whenever one of us girls would be sad or depressed—even when she was feeling just as bad—she'd be the first one to pick us up and set us in the right direction. Always making sure we were moving forward. Always.

She's an incredibly strong woman. I don't know how she did it. But I know I couldn't have survived without her.

And those lessons my mom taught me so long ago, when we were struggling every day to make ends meet, when a man that I loved and she loved slowly died and there was nothing anyone could do about it—those lessons stayed with me. Even today, I know that if I were to live in the past, I wouldn't be where I am in the present. If I spent my time dwelling on all the terrible things that have happened to me (and yes—fair warning!—there are more to come), I would fall into a really bad place. Like a black hole. And I just can't do that.

I won't do that.

Mom has taught me to just keep looking ahead to all the incredible opportunities. Amazingly, those opportunities actually appeared, even though I had no idea what form they would take or what they would be.

I just knew they were out there. Somewhere.

CHAPTER 4

SCHOOL DAYS

You never know how strong
you are until being strong is
the only choice you have.

—UNKNOWN

High school is typically the place where you figure
out what you're going to do with your life—or at
least get some idea of where you fit in the world. Are you
gonna go to college? Learn a trade? Get married and start
having kids?

Play video games in your parents' basement?

My school, Bowman High School, had like 125 kids
in the entire school. I think there were 30 people in my
graduating class.

For me, school didn't offer any answers, it just brought
up more questions. It's not that my classes were hard for
me, it was just hard to sit through them without becoming
insanely bored. I wanted to learn about something that

excited me, that gave me that feeling of, "Yes! That's what I want to do." But nothing felt like it fit.

I didn't feel like *I* fit.

The one thing in my life that really made me happy, where I really felt like I was awake and alive and firing on all my cylinders, was when I was working.

It started when I landed my very first job (besides cleaning the shit barn!) as a paper route girl, delivering the local paper a few times a week. I'll never forget my first paycheck. I slept with it under my pillow the night I got it. It was a little less than $100, but it might as well have been $1,000, or a million. I never felt so empowered before. After a childhood spent feeling like I couldn't control anything, here, finally, was something I could do.

I was so proud to have made my own money! To be able to do it on my own, and not have to ask anyone for help or put any more pressure on my family. It was like I discovered this amazing secret.

From then on, I worked as much as I could doing anything and everything I could. I babysat at night, and in the summer, I did it full-time. I worked at the local Radio Shack (which has since closed) after school and on weekends.

But the job that really changed my life was at The Grapevine.

I remember I was in around 8th or 9th grade. And this women whose husband was a teacher at our school came by after school looking for kids interested in helping put together the booklet for that year's rodeo.

The annual rodeo was a huge, giant, massive deal in our town. Like Bowman's Super Bowl. So there were like thousands of these little booklets this woman—her name was Betty—needed folded and stapled together.

I was in.

My job was folding pages with this pain-in-the-ass folder machine that always jammed up. But I stuck with it, and Betty stuck with me. Being a curious one (yes, even about manual labor), I was always asking if I could help with other projects Betty needed to deal with. So she started letting me do binding—books, notepads and anything else that needed to be collated. I cut business cards and packaged them. Eventually, she let me work on the computer laying out paper newsletters, which was fun.

And I learned how to use an Apple computer. You know, those old ones with a floppy disk?

They only had IBM computers at school, so I kind of felt like a big shot using an Apple computer!!

I loved all of it at The Grapevine, actually. There was always a big project to conquer. And I loved working for Betty.

I think I worked there from 8th grade through my senior year.

But still—I wanted more challenges to tackle.

THE LIFEGUARD CHALLENGE

I've always loved to swim. I taught myself (naturally!), I never had any formal training, but I was pretty good at it. And the summer before 10th grade, I decided that I was going to spend that summer in the pool—working as a swim teacher and a lifeguard.

I begged my mom to drive me the 2½ hours to Bismarck to get certified—which was the only way I could legally work as a lifeguard. Of course, this cost money—a lot of money. And it didn't sound like the most brilliant use of our limited funds to my mom. Honestly, what were my chances of making it? All the people I would be swimming with were from bigger schools, in bigger towns, with formal lessons and swim teams and all the things Bowman didn't have.

What if I spent the money and I didn't pass?

I was determined to try. I walked in, took the hardest classes in the classroom and in the water of my entire life, and passed with both my teaching degree and my lifeguard degree.

My mom about died.

So every summer from then on, I worked at the pool, Radio Shack and The Grapevine—in addition to cleaning the shit barn!

You would think this would have told me something about myself. That I was a fast learner and a hard worker. That I was flexible. That I really, really loved everything about working and would ultimately be able to succeed at lots of different things.

But back at school, that didn't crystallize into any sort of Vision for my Future. I didn't fit in to any of the normal boxes.

Our school offered a special program where everybody got to "shadow" a professional for a day. You would follow a local businessperson like doctor, or a lawyer, or a teacher, to get an idea of what their daily life was all about.

There wasn't anyone in the town of Bowman—or anywhere near Bowman—that I was remotely interested in shadowing (other than Betty—of course!).

I didn't want to be a doctor, or a lawyer, or a teacher— or any of the typical jobs offered in Bowman. But the people at Bowman High were really nice, and got approval for me to go over an hour away to Dickinson, where I got to shadow an interior designer.

I loved design, but I guess there wasn't a huge demand for professional decorators back home in Bowman!

LIVING DIFFERENT

There was really no one else like me in high school. I was kind of the "all work and no play" girl. That's what I was known for—in the yearbook, I think I was voted "hardest worker." I was friends with everyone, but had no specific circle, because I didn't participate in activities like most of them did. I got to do my one sport a year—one year it was basketball, one year it was track, one year it was softball, one year it was golf—but I couldn't afford to hang out with the other kids who played sports and did activities all year long.

So I felt different.

I had one best friend, Melissa, who I hung out with a lot. She was probably the only person who knew everything about my family (and loved me unconditionally anyway). Everyone else knew bits and pieces—like that we were poor, or that I didn't have a dad—that just made me feel even more different.

Another reason I felt different was the fact that I didn't party. There's not a whole lot to do in a small town, and for a lot of high school kids, partying is basically the only source of recreation. Hey, it is even in towns where there are tons of things to do! But after what I had seen happen to my dad, alcohol was just terrifying to me. I don't think I even tried it until my senior year party or that following summer.

I was friends with everyone, but fit in nowhere.

Well, there was one place I did fit in—with my stepbrother Brady.

Because he didn't fit in either.

We saw each other every day, obviously, since we lived together—Bob had full custody of Brady during high school. Sometimes that level of closeness was hard, but usually it was fun.

Brady was one of those kids who falls through the cracks in the system a little bit because he was different. So many people left him behind—teachers, neighbors, friends. It was incredibly disheartening to see. He could have been something. I knew it. But no one else could see it.

I couldn't believe there were so many mean people.

But there were fun times too.

I remember the nights we'd get to go out. (One night a week and only until 9PM! Another one of Bob's crazy rules.) I'd normally get home before curfew because I was terrified to be late—a trait I've carried with me to this day. But Brady liked to push the envelope. He was always just on time...or just a little late.

Later, he would wake me up, come sit on the edge of my bed in the dark and tell me all about his day.

He was a talker. Sometimes I just wanted to sleep, other times, we laughed. I loved those moments.

But my favorite moment with Brady had to be our last shit-barn-funded vacation together. It was the summer after our sophomore year, so all the other kids were gone, and Bob, my mom, Brady and I drove our van all the way to Alaska. Which, it turns out, is a very long drive! When we got there, Bob and Brady got to go charter fishing and caught a 25-pound salmon (which, in Bob-speak, was about $200 worth of fish!).

It was an amazing adventure for all of us.

Oh—there was one more, really important person in my life during those years. My boyfriend, Mark. We were together from when I was a freshman until after graduation. He was really funny and silly—we hung out a lot, and I really loved him. We even got engaged.

But by the time high school was over, things had changed a lot for me. And not in a very good way.

GOODBYE AGAIN

When something bad happens you have three choices. You can either let it define you, let it destroy you, or you can let it strengthen you.

—UNKNOWN

My sister Jess graduated from high school in 1999—my freshman year, and we had a party at our house at the end of May to celebrate. All of our family and close friends were there. And the biggest moment had to be when our half-brother Sheldon pulled up.

We were all so excited to see him—we all ran out of the house and practically tackled him. It was an awesome moment.

That was the last time I saw him. He died that Memorial Day Weekend.

He and two friends were at a party at the local dam—a lot of people used to go camping there and party on the weekends. Well, even though they'd all been drinking, Sheldon and his buddies hopped in a pickup truck. Sheldon was on the passenger side, there was one guy in the middle, and one guy driving.

They were going too fast and missed a turn—right outside my hometown.

The guy that was sitting in the middle survived. I've heard that my brother and the driver saved his life. They were both big guys and they must have acted like airbags or something, keeping him from being thrown from the truck.

My brother and the driver weren't so lucky.

Once again, we were in mourning. Losing our dad was awful. Then losing our oldest brother who reminded us so much of our dad…it was like reliving it all over again. And my grandparents…I honestly don't know how they held it together.

The funeral was really special. Sheldon had this car he loved so much—I think it was a Camaro. They parked it next to the funeral home and everyone put roses on it and wrote notes to him. Then, after the funeral, his brother and both of my sisters and I hopped in it and drove it out to the cemetery.

But first, we had to start the car with pliers.

So we all wound up crying and laughing at the same time, all the way to the cemetery.

There was a little memorial by the accident scene for years after it happened. Every single time I drove through that area I had to be reminded. It was tough.

And to be honest, everything was tough. I felt like I was cursed—like my whole family was cursed. One horrible thing after another was happening to me. I didn't know anyone that had been through even, like, an ounce of the shit my family had to deal with. No one understood what we were going through. Even we didn't understand it. No one knew what to say.

I remember the school counselor meeting with me and asking if I was okay, and I was like, "Hell no, I'm not okay."

But what could I do? When even the professionals didn't have any idea how to help me? It was just shitty all the way around.

But Sheldon's death also inspired something that would end up being the biggest success in my life for some time.

I was part of a group in high school called FCCLA, which stands for Family, Career and Community Leaders of America. We had to pair up in groups and do something impactful in our community as a project. So I paired up with my friend Ashley. And, given what happened to Sheldon, I knew exactly what we could do.

We decided to have a "Ghost Out."

A "Ghost Out" is a way of dramatizing the fact that every 90 seconds, someone in America dies in a drunk driving accident. That day, with the school's approval, we took turns sitting by the school intercom. And every 90 seconds, representing the moment another person would die, we'd call out a name of a student at our school. Then we'd paint that person's face white, and for the rest of the day, no one would be allowed to talk to them.

Anyone who had a white face was "dead" due to drunk driving.

By the end of the day, the majority of the kids at our school had white faces. Then the principal called everyone into the gym, and we got up in front of everyone and explained what we had just done and what it meant. I told everyone the story of my brother Sheldon and the impact drinking and driving had on my life, personally.

The presentation was rated strongly enough that our school chapter of FCCLA was sent to the state competition to present there. When we presented to friends at our school that was one thing. But heading into the state competition, something changed for me.

I realized, "I want to win this shit."

Not just because I wanted to be the best, but because the Nationals were in Anaheim, California. Home of Disneyland. A free trip.

Not something a girl like me got to experience every day.

So we got up there and killed it—we beat everyone else in the state of North Dakota. That meant we would move to Nationals, and got to make the trip to Anaheim. I had never been on a plane before.

I threw up the entire way to California!

(I'm much better at flying now).

The presentation was pretty emotional. I remember standing in front of the judging panel talking about the accident and the brother I lost, just bawling my head off.

But once I started talking it got easier.

And we won.

Out of all the kids in the competition, from all over the country, these kids from this dinky little high school in the middle of nowhere in North Dakota came out on top.

Which meant we had to get on stage in front of thousands of people to accept our award—definitely the first time I had ever experienced anything like that. Plus, we got to go to Disneyland. Which was definitely the most fun I had that year.

By a long shot.

After that summer came my senior year, and I was definitely excited. High school was finally coming to an end, and it couldn't have been soon enough for me.

On night in October, I was out driving around and saw my brother Brady driving with some friends in his car. I pulled up next to him and he told me they were all going to Dickinson. He invited me to come along.

Knowing Bob and his curfew craziness, I didn't think this was such a good idea, so I said no to joining the group for the drive to Dickinson. I also remember telling Brady, "I don't think you should; you probably won't be home by curfew if you do."

Brady said, "No, no, I'll be home by curfew."

So I was like, "Well make sure."

That was the last conversation we ever had.

He took the back roads home that night and was going too fast in a curve.

There were five kids in the car. Three of them died, including Brady.

It was just too much for me to handle.

From that day on, I had to go to school every day without him, finishing out my senior year with this empty desk in the class, reminding me. Like I wouldn't have been reminded anyway. But it just made it that much harder.

It was visible. Every day. Right in my face.

Back at home, this last tragedy pushed my mom and Bob too far. They decided they had to get away, out of Bowman. Bob was building a house a couple of hours away in the hills—he was a carpenter and was able to do it for very little money—and he and my mom just turned all their attention to this house. I guess as a way of dealing with their grief.

So there I was: turning 18, my sisters had moved out, my dad died, my half-brother died, now my stepbrother who was also one of my closest friends just died.

And my parents were so devastated, they had kind of stopped participating in my life. At least, at that time.

It wasn't their fault. I don't blame them by any means. But I was in so much pain, I couldn't help screaming inside, "This happened to me, too. I lost someone, too. Throw me a bone here."

Not that I would ever tell them that.

I was incredibly numb. I still am today about it, really. How can you even process something like that?

Still, even though I was numb, I was also so, so angry. Our lives were so bad it was like fiction—like a story someone made up where horrible things keep happening and happening, over and over again.

Sometimes I would wonder, "Is there even a freakin' God? And if so, what the Hell did we do to get the ass end of the deal? We're good people. Why??"

It was my deepest low. It was so bad, I really wasn't all that interested in waking up the next day. And what killed me the most was that Brady had been cheated out of a regular life. The school system sucked at helping him, his friends were mean…he had the roughest time and I felt like everyone failed him.

They didn't get him. They didn't get why he was different.

But I did.

Brady and Sheldon's deaths really changed me. They shook my faith in life to the core. Actually, they shook my faith in more than life—in God, in fate, in everything. The world just seemed totally random and totally horrible.

As you can probably imagine, there weren't a whole lot of high points during my senior year. But after all the struggles, I was still really excited about graduating. Not that I had any real plans for after graduation, but at least

high school would be over and I would be able to start a
new chapter in my life.

I just had no idea what I was going to do with it.

My mom and Bob were still overcome with grief—
and building their house two hours away. So they weren't
really thinking about my future. Of course, there was no
money for college even if they were.

But graduation was still supposed to be special.

Well, it was special, but maybe not in the way I wanted.
Part of the ceremony was dedicated to honoring Brady.
Each member of my class walked up to Mom and Bob
and gave them a rose. It was so, so sad. It was incredibly
moving and showed pure love from my graduating class.
But it also turned my graduation into a memorial for my
brother.

Instead of being a happy celebration, it was the saddest
day ever.

My graduation party wasn't much better. It was held in
the middle of my mom and Bob moving out of the house.
While we were all eating dinner, people were loading up
the washer and dryer.

It pretty much summed up the state of my life.

PART 2

LEARNING THE ROPES

CHAPTER 5

ON MY OWN

Running away from your problems
is a race you'll never win.

—UNKNOWN

Right around graduation, my boyfriend Mark and I were driving down to South Dakota. Suddenly, he pulled over to the side of the road. He said he wanted to "look at something."

Next thing I knew, he was down on one knee, asking me to marry him.

And of course, I said yes.

I had no idea what I was going to do with my life after high school, and getting married just seemed like the logical next step. It's what people who had boyfriends did after high school. And Mark had been my boyfriend forever, stood by me through all the hell I went through, and had proven over and over again what a good man he was.

He really was a great guy.

I was super excited about the idea of getting married. After so much yuck in my life, I was just so excited for something—anything. A change. A new life. Just something where I could get out of where I had been for so long.

He worked hard, loved me, I got to have a wedding and be a bride and dress up, what more could you want?

Right after I graduated, we got an apartment together closer to where my parents had moved in South Dakota. I was excited about a new town, living with my boyfriend… something, anything different.

My family was a little worried…of course they knew and liked Mark, but I was so young. At that time—and I think when anyone is that young—I was all caught up in the idea of "love." It was so much fun imagining our lives together, the kids we'd have and all that kind of stuff. We'd been together for four years already, so of course I thought we'd be together forever.

We didn't last the summer.

I just got freaked out by it all. It was still an incredibly difficult time in my life. All that happened my senior year, losing Brady, everything my mom and Bob were going through, trying to "find myself" in the middle of all this turmoil…I was just a mess.

I probably did everything I shouldn't have done in a relationship. And inside, I just kept feeling myself wanting to break away from everyone and everything.

To get out of town. To get away from myself.

The unfortunate thing is that I ruined "us." It wasn't him. It was all me. I was in an incredibly dark place in my life.

By the end of the summer I had moved into my own apartment, was working at The Gap, and helping my aunt and uncle in their business. None of this was meant to be permanent by any means—I was just trying to get my life back together and figure out what I wanted to do, where I wanted to go.

Just any sign that would lead me in a different direction.

I knew I didn't want to be where I was, doing what I was doing, but I had no idea how to do anything else. So I thought, I'll just go to college like the rest of the people my age. I started going to a local college in South Dakota, taking general electives, with no real idea what I wanted to do. Nothing really excited me. Nothing clicked.

Then Bob and I came up with an interesting idea...

ANCHORS AWAY!

Bob had spent several years in the Marines when he was younger. In the military, he got to travel, see new places, got to live and eat for free, plus he was paid to develop skills—all at the same time!

It sounded like the perfect solution for me.

So we went and met with all the military outlets. My first choice had been the Air Force, but they told me I would probably be stationed in the U.S., and I wanted to see the world. I wanted to get as far away as possible from what I knew, to travel and go to other countries and just be part of something bigger than myself.

So we tried the Navy. And hit the jackpot. They promised me a future that sounded exciting and fulfilling, plus they gave me the best offer and the best sign-on bonus. So I thought, what the heck?

I signed on the dotted line. I was going to be a sailor.

Right after Thanksgiving they shipped me off to Chicago. I was so excited. The big city! I thought, "I have arrived! I'm going to CHICAGO!!"

Well…turns out it was actually a bit north of Chicago. They bussed us from the Chicago airport up north to their boot camp. I'll never forget getting off that bus. It was cold, it was dark, and—like most of the very young, very unsuspecting people with me—I had no idea what was about to happen.

It turned out that what was going to happen…was screaming.

As soon as we stepped off the bus, people started yelling and screaming at us. We weren't lining up right, we weren't standing up straight, we weren't listening to instructions, we packed too much, we used the bathroom too much (that was when I first learned NEVER to call the bathroom a bathroom. It's a head.). Whatever we did, it was wrong, and it was pretty much the worst thing a person could ever, ever, possibly do.

I was scared out of my mind.

To be totally honest, I really, really wanted my mom.

The soldiers went through all of our stuff and made us put everything we came with in a box, which they then sent back to our families. It would have been nice if they'd told us not to bother to pack all that stuff in the first place, but what fun would that have been? So much more fulfilling to watch us part with all of our earthly possessions in person...

Then, with my entire wardrobe in a box heading west, it was time for new clothes. We stood in a line for our new Navy outfits. You know, the shoes, the uniform, the sweats, the running shoes. And what outfits they were. Seriously. The ugliest clothes ever. Like they were specifically designed to make you look bad.

And then, the worst thing happened.

They cut all my hair off.

Now, I'm not a super-vain kind of girl. I'm kind of a tomboy. But I did have pretty great hair. It was longer, and blonde, and nice enough to earn me the Best Hair title in high school (along with Hardest Worker, and I think, if I remember correctly, Best Legs?).

Well, they had us all wait in line (it seemed like we were always waiting in line for one thing or another), and when it was my turn, they just cut my hair right off.

Snip! It was gone.

Looking back, I think the hardest part of the whole thing was that I had absolutely no idea it was coming. It was like I was having an out of body experience—thinking holy shit, is this really happening? How can they do this? And then, when I saw myself, I didn't even recognize who I was.

I looked like a boy. A very scared, sad boy.

Next, we got our bunk list—I had a top bunk—and learned the strict schedule we would have to adhere to if we were going to survive with a minimal amount of yelling and screaming and abuse. No one really talked—everyone was a little freaked out.

By the end of my first day, I knew I'd made a terrible mistake. It was so scary, feeling ugly, in a new place, surrounded by cranky people…I wanted to die! Instead of enlisting in the military, I felt like I'd volunteered for Hell.

From then on, every day went pretty much like this. We'd wake up way too early in the morning, shower with a bunch of girls, get dressed, make our beds and shine our shoes—and it all had to be done perfectly in like 10 minutes. If your shoes weren't shined just right, they'd make you sit there in front of everyone and shine your shoes again while they yelled at you the entire time about what an idiot you were.

We'd spend the day running like a billion miles, stopping to eat horrible food during these short, timed breaks, and then repeating it all over again. Plus there were the extra jobs. Newbies got picked on a lot, and since I was a newbie, I had to do the most disgusting jobs. It was kind of like the shit barn back in Bowman, except there was no fun family vacation waiting at the end. Just more shit work.

It just sucked every which way.

Now, just to be clear, I am in no way disparaging the military as a whole. I have nothing but respect for people who go through boot camp and actually survive, and get tougher, and become leaders, and all that stuff you're supposed to do. The problem was, boot camp is designed to "break" you so they can build you back up again. But after everything I'd experienced in my short life, I was already broken. Seriously broken. To go to a place where every minute of every day would be dedicated to breaking me more...well, as you can imagine, it was a lot to take.

But I did my best to work hard (something I'm good at) and keep my head down and try to avoid as much abuse as I could. And weeks went by of this ugly, horrible new life, and it was all pretty awful, but I was surviving.

Until I did something wrong.

I can't for the life of me remember what it was. Maybe I didn't fold my clothes the right way (even though I had worked at The Gap—where folding a t-shirt is a complex art form) or maybe my bed sheets weren't tight enough to bounce a quarter off of. I have no idea.

But whatever it was, it meant Abuse Chelsea Time had officially begun.

First, I got called to attention. Then my Chief Petty Officer walked up to me and spit on my shoes. Then the cussing started—an endless stream of curse words all with basically one message: that I was a completely worthless human being who did not deserve to live.

I knew right then and there that I couldn't do it. I needed to go home. But how? You can't just quit the military like a job. They don't really care if you're not happy—you're not supposed to be happy in boot camp! You pretty much need to move mountains to get out.

I used my one, allotted weekly four-minute phone call to call my mom. I told her what was happening, and basically begged her to please, please find a way to get me the hell out of there.

And—amazingly—she came through for me.

Somehow, she got to someone somewhere with the power to save me. She told him what was happening, and I think her words were basically, "If you don't get my daughter out of there, I will come there and get her myself."

Thank God for that.

That next morning, I was pulled out of my bunk and put in a room with a few people like me. You know... other curious ones. The people that weren't fitting in in the Navy, that wanted to go home, that were sick or had some other problem. And they told us that not only were we getting out, we weren't even going to be punished! We were getting "honorably discharged."

It was like a big ol' party! To say we were happy would be a massive understatement.

Unfortunately, the whole discharging process takes some time, so I was there through Christmas and didn't actually get home until the beginning of the next year.

All in all, my military career lasted about 35 days.

When it was finally over, they put me on a train to Chicago, then a bus to South Dakota, and when I got to my stop my parents were there to meet me. I don't think I was ever so thankful to see them. I slept for days after that.

But then I woke up. And it was the beginning of 2003, and I was back in a small town, single, staying with my parents...and trying to figure out what to do next.

Eventually, I got an apartment and found a job I thought was great—at Wells Fargo bank. And from January through August of that year, I dedicated myself to getting back on track again. I worked full-time at Wells Fargo, I worked at a steak house at night and waitressed, and helped my aunt and uncle in their business that summer when I could. It wasn't exciting, I wasn't seeing the world (or even another state!), but I wasn't getting screamed at on a daily basis either.

At the time, it felt like a win.

LOVE & MARRIAGE: PART 1

And in the end, we were all just humans, drunk on the idea that love, only love, could heal our brokenness.

—F. SCOTT FITZGERALD

I was living in a town called Sturgis, South Dakota—home of the annual Sturgis Motorcycle Rally. Which is a pretty big deal. Thousands of people come to this little town in the middle of nowhere from all over the country.

One of them was a guy from Illinois named Bart.

No, not Simpson.

When a friend introduced us, I was pretty excited. I hadn't dated anyone in a long time. Luckily, my hair had grown back and I no longer looked like a boy. And we wound up hitting it off.

I don't remember why, exactly. I think the idea of a man paying attention to me at that point in my life was probably enough.

He went home after the rally and we did the long-distance thing for a while, traveling back and forth to see each other. But it didn't take long before I put two and two together and realized that my new man was the perfect solution to my old wanderlust.

He asked me to marry him. And I moved to Illinois.

My mom wasn't happy. At all. Not just that I was moving to Illinois, but that I was getting married to a guy I'd practically just met, that we knew very little about (except that he was a cowboy) and that she and the rest of my family weren't a fan of. There was a lot of that, "Are you sure you want to go through with this?" kind of thing.

But I wasn't worried.

I kissed her goodbye and assured her I'd be fine. I was so excited to go to another state and live in a new place I'd never been. Maybe more excited than I was about the getting married part.

I moved to Illinois in the fall of 2003, started working at a bank full-time and taking college classes, still with no idea what I really wanted to do or needed to be studying. But for all my desire to get away, it turned out I missed my mom. So right before we were supposed to get married, I quit the bank and the classes and we moved back to South Dakota.

Bart got a job working on a farm. We lived in the little tiny farm house that they build on the farm for the hired hand. Since we were in the middle of nowhere, I started taking online classes, trying to figure out what I wanted to do, or be.

The wedding was that August at my parents' cabin. Of course, I still didn't have any money and my parents didn't have any money to contribute, so it wasn't a big, elaborate party or anything. But I did get a dress and I had bridesmaids and it was outdoors.

As soon as it was over, it was back to real life. We didn't even have a honeymoon.

The marriage lasted less than six months.

It was obvious pretty much right away that being stuck in a tiny little house in the middle of nowhere was not the life I dreamed of. Bart figured out pretty quick that I was not happy or satisfied. So when I left, he was not surprised. He was out of town, I just packed everything up and moved in with a friend, and he came home to an empty house. But he knew it was coming. He didn't try and fight it or anything. I filed for divorce and he signed the papers. We spoke a few times after that as friends, and that was it.

At the age of 20, I was already a divorcee.

HOW BILL O'REILLY SAVED MY LIFE

At some point during my brief marriage, my life changed pretty dramatically. It gave me something other than being somebody's wife to think about. I found out about a job as an account manager at a company called One World Direct—a call center and global distribution company which happened to be one of the only viable companies located in the part of South Dakota where I lived, in a little town of 2,500 called Mobridge.

And I set my sights on getting that job—no matter what.

I don't know why, but just knowing that position was out there lit a fire under me. Something told me that I could do it, that if I could just get my foot in the door, I could build some kind of career for myself.

But getting that foot in that particular door was a major challenge.

After all, I was pretty much still fresh out of high school, with a failed military career (that no one knew about!) and some college work under my belt.

But I wasn't going to let a little thing like being a 19-year-old military deserter, soon-to-be divorcee and non-college-graduate stop me. I applied for the account manager job three or four times, and when I didn't hear back, I actually went to the owner's office and asked if the position was still open—at least twice.

I guess I was stalking him. But in a completely harmless way—I swear!

I was pretty persistent. The owner of the company once told my mom, "Wherever I went, there she was." And, like the old saying goes, persistence pays off. Even if it takes the form of stalking.

He finally broke down and hired me.

It wasn't for the job I applied for. I didn't get to be an account manager, he started me as a customer service representative. But I might as well have been a Senior VP at that point, I was so, so happy. I made like $10.00 an hour and I got benefits—benefits!—I felt like a real professional for the first time. After moving out on Bart and living with my friend for a while, I was able to get my own apartment in town and take care of myself.

The job itself was not what you might consider a glamorous position worth stalking someone over. It basically consisted of answering phones for One World's clients—one of whom was Fox TV legend Bill O'Reilly—when people would call in to order products marketed by those clients.

But I really enjoyed it. And not just the feeling of having a "real job" with benefits, but the work itself.

Every day was different. Every call was different. One of our clients sold these special vitamins that protect your eyes from macular degeneration—so I would end up having these long, painfully hilarious conversations with old people who couldn't hear anything I said. I learned how to speak very slowly, clearly, and most importantly, LOUDLY!

Then I'd get a Bill O'Reilly call and ask, "Do you want to buy the 'No Spin' towel and doormat?" I knew I was just answering phones and facilitating orders. I knew I wasn't changing anyone's life—except maybe helping some of those old people see a little better.

But I was so proud to work at One World, and I met some of the most incredible people while working there. I got to hang out with people that loved me like family every single day. It wasn't just about working hard and having my own career, but to finally, after so much hardship and loss, have friends and good people around me. To get to laugh, and make small talk, and experience actual joy on a daily basis.

One World saved me. I had finally found a place where I belonged.

CHAPTER 6

"HOW CAN I HELP?"

It is only when we decide that ordinary is an insult, that we become the exquisite miracles we were born to be.

—GREGSON

It wasn't long before I was totally rocking it at One World. Which might not sound like much to you—most people who've never experienced a call center have this idea in their head that the work is the kind of no-brainer stuff that anyone can do. After all, how hard can it be, answering the phone and making sure the person on the other end gets their Bill O'Reilly "No Spin Zone" doormat?

Well, in reality, it's actually pretty complex.

There were so many companies that distributed their products through One World, I needed to know everything about every single one of them and keep them all straight in my brain. Because I had to be able to answer questions on any one of those companies at any given time when someone called to order something. A person calling to order eye vitamins likely had no interest at all in a Bill O'Reilly "No Spin Zone" doormat. So it was definitely not what I'd call easy.

Although, after a while, it did become easy for me…

I just had a knack for it. Maybe it was because I'd always liked helping people, and now that's essentially what I was doing all day, every day, and getting paid for it! So, even though I was young, and new, and didn't have a college degree yet, I started emerging as a leader. Soon I was mentoring and training other newbies.

Then my curiosity kicked in—how can I make this process easier for everyone? I created documentation processes to help as the call center was growing, and then taught them to my co-workers. It was such a rush. For the first time, I felt needed and smart—I even got a little raise right away. Woohoo! Go me!

But once that was all under control, my curiosity kicked in again. I loved helping people and teaching them, but that didn't stop me from starting to feel just the tiniest bit bored.

I had been at One World for about a year when I saw my chance to change that.

I found out that the bookkeeper—who had been with the company from the very beginning—was leaving to pursue other opportunities. She had given her notice, and One World basically had two weeks to fill this position.

Had I ever done bookkeeping before? Hell no! But I wasn't going to let that stop me.

I walked into the CEO's office and said, "I hear you need some help with bookkeeping. I'd be glad to fill in while you find a replacement." He said he'd think about it.

I started training the next day.

I had about two weeks to spend shadowing the woman who was leaving to learn how to do the books for this fairly big company. I had never done this kind of work before in my entire life. But that didn't intimidate me. I understood numbers and the basic principles of what a bookkeeper was supposed to do, and since I'd figured out so much on the job at the call center just by doing it, I was pretty sure I could figure this out too.

But just in case, I went on Amazon.com and bought a copy of *Bookkeeping for Dummies.*

After about two weeks, the training period was over and I became the company bookkeeper. I was only supposed to hold this position until they found a *real* bookkeeper as a replacement. But they must not have been looking very hard, because I ended up in the position for six very looooong months.

I definitely didn't enjoy the job. Just working with numbers all day did not excite or stimulate me.

Let's just say my curiosity with bookkeeping was satisfied rather quickly.

But it was a calculated move. I knew I could do it. I knew I was helping them. I knew I was making myself indispensable. And most importantly, I knew it was a step up. That was huge for me...I wanted to keep going, keep climbing the ladder, keep getting better titles and proving myself. So I stuck it out, while keeping my eyes and ears open for what I might do next. I definitely didn't want to go back to the call center.

I was looking for my next step up.

CLIMBING THE LADDER

When they finally brought in a new bookkeeper for me to train, I had scoped out a couple of new opportunities. From my vantage point, I saw that One World needed help in the tech department and in the Account Management department.

So of course, I told the CEO that I could do both.

They put me to work helping manage the CSRs—the Customer Service Reps—who worked answering phones like I used to. It was kind of strange. I was in charge of people who were much, much older than me—I was still in my early 20s and they were probably in their 30s, 40s, and 50s. Sometimes I felt like they didn't take me seriously, like they still saw me as this super-eager 19-year-old kid who had talked her way into the job. But I just kept going.

That's around when I met Justin.

New beginnings are often disguised as painful endings.

—LAO TZU

I had gone out to dinner with some friends from work and was introduced to a local guy who all the girls seemed to know except me. Which I guess is typical in a town of 2500 people. If there's a single guy out there, all the girls are going to know who he is and what his deets are.

Justin lived about 15 miles away from Mobridge on his dad's ranch in Selby, where he also worked. We hit it off right away—maybe because a part of me was always looking for love, and Justin was ready to provide it. He was super nice and super sweet, with a big heart. And he was willing to take it slow and move at my pace instead of rushing into the whole marriage thing again.

I was so thankful I met a guy that was nice and good to me…and that was just the medicine I needed to be okay with myself in my own shoes again.

Meanwhile, back at One World, I discovered something new about myself—it turned out I was incredibly technical. Unlike bookkeeping, which, to be honest, kind of put me to sleep, I really, really liked working with computers. And I found a huge ally in the company's Chief Technical Officer (CTO), a guy named Stewart.

Stewart saw that I was interested in technology, and he made it his mission to help me succeed. Of course, being curious me, it wasn't long before I asked him, "Is there anything I can do to help on the side, while I'm helping with the call center, to work on technology?"

He put me to work analyzing data. And they actually gave me a very professional-sounding title—Data Analyst.

At the same time, over in the call center, I noticed One World could really use some help with account management. So, back I went to the CEO's office to report my findings—and, of course, to tell him I wanted the job. And since it was easier for them to hire an account manager from Customer Service, who already knew all the accounts, than to bring in someone from the outside and have them start from scratch, I had another new title— Account Manager.

So I now was basically working three jobs—Customer Service Manager, Data Analyst and Account Manager.

As an Account Manager, instead of taking calls for Bill O'Reilly, I was helping manage the Bill O'Reilly account!

Well, actually, there were four of us splitting account management duties, since there were so many accounts to manage. The job was all about logistics—managing products, managing fulfillment and coordinating with the clients. Basically I was responsible for getting the stuff and making sure it got out. And I kept training people, because sharing what I knew was just a part of who I was.

And who I am.

Between my work as an Account Manager/Trainer and as a Data Analyst, I felt like I had the best of both worlds. I was so excited to be moving up the ladder again, to have those new, more important sounding titles. And then there was the money. I was probably making about $17 an hour, which felt like a six-figure salary for a girl my age, from my background, in small town South Dakota. They even gave me little bonuses every once in a while, which made life even sweeter. All those money worries from my childhood were definitely a thing of the past. There would be no food stamps, no low-income housing, no donated turkeys for me.

I was living large.

But what was even more important to me was how competent, how smart, how just freakin' great I felt. After growing up wondering where I fit in and what I was going to do with my life, I was part of a business that I knew like the back of my hand. I understood almost every facet of how it ran. I could probably answer any question on behalf of the company. Spending two and a half years with One World earned me what felt like a PhD. I felt like an expert.

Of course, not everyone felt that way about me. I moved up in the company really quickly and had a lot of responsibility. But I couldn't help noticing, even at this point, that a lot of people still treated me like I was a newbie in the call center! They didn't look at me as a leader. They didn't act like, "Wow, Chelsea—she's done incredible work." I felt a little bit used—almost like a tool sometimes. I was being paid better than most people my age, but I knew that if I were older, or had a college degree, or didn't still look like a 20-year-old, I'd be making more. I knew I was worthy of more.

I was worthy of respect.

But I knew the only way to get that respect, if I was ever going to get it (which didn't seem likely, to be honest), was to continue on the path that I was on, working hard and staying curious for the next opportunity, and pouncing on it the minute it popped up. Because, as I had learned, no one was going to come and offer it to me!

CLIMBING HIGHER

At some point along the line, after about a year of dating, Justin and I got engaged. I don't really remember how it happened, it was something we had talked about and knew we were going to do. We had talked about raising a family and the life we would have together. So when we made the decision, I remember feeling like, "Yay, now it's time to get on with my life, a family, career..."

Maybe career wasn't supposed to be something I was thinking about when I was getting engaged?

Eventually, I rented a house for us in Selby and we moved in together. It was better to live in Selby, because he needed to be close to the ranch, and because I was helping him get a job there doing road work for the state.

But even when we were living together, I just kind of kept putting things off. Most girls my age planned their weddings way ahead of time, down to the tiniest detail—reading bridal magazines and picking dresses and daydreaming about their "big day." But I was so excited by my life at One World, that's where all my creative energy went. I was planning my career, not my wedding. I never even set a date! People kept asking me when the wedding would be, or how excited I was about it, and I just...wasn't so into it.

Looking back, maybe that should have been a sign.

At One World, my career was moving as fast as my wedding plans were not. I moved out of account management and went 100% into the tech department. Technically I was still a data analyst, but I was doing a lot of different reporting for the company, in terms of looking at our numbers and planning for the future. I started working solely for Stewart, and I absolutely loved it. It got me in this really technical mindset, and I learned SO MUCH about running a business, online businesses, products, etc. It was super fun.

But of course, I was still curious...

Around this time, I noticed One World needed help with sales. Like, serious help. The VP of sales just had another baby and already had two very small kids. She was a little distracted, a little busy, and as a result, the sales calls that were coming in weren't being answered as quickly as usual.

So I started taking them without making a big deal about it. You know, I was just...helping...

Then one day, it hit me. I'm doing sales—and I love this! I loved the energy. I loved the rush of making the sale. It was like a drug for me, and I was totally and completely addicted. So once again, I marched back into the executive office, this time to ask the Ops/VP of Sales if they'd be interested in me working in the sales department. Oh, and since I'd been learning so much working for Stewart, could I also work on some business development for the company?

I didn't ask for any more money. I didn't even ask for commission because, at this point, I didn't exactly understand what commission was or how it worked.

Is it really any surprise that they said yes?

But, to be honest, I didn't care about the money. I was just so eager to SELL—I jumped right into it the second they gave me the go-ahead. And, almost instantly, I was killing it. Seriously—I sold more in a short period of time than anyone had at One World, like, ever. So much that for the first time, I was getting noticed for what I did. Instead of thinking, "Oh, how cute, little Chelsea's trying something new," everyone was like "HOLY COW LOOK AT HER!!!!"

I had definitely found my calling.

I was crushing it. Bringing on more clients than they knew what to do with. Eventually, I worked on my technique and learned how to pull back a little bit and refine my process. Instead of signing just anyone up because I knew I could close them (which is sales language for getting them to buy), I started being more thoughtful about exactly who we were closing. I was also able to create my own processes, create the proposals and draw up the contracts. But more than anything, I sold, baby!

And—oh yeah—somewhere in the midst of all of this, I finally got married.

LOVE & MARRIAGE: PART 2

It takes two, two sides to every story.
I admit half of it, I'm not that innocent.
I face my demons. I paid my dues.
I had to grow up, I wish you could too.
I wanted to save you,
but I can only save myself.

— PERRY

Somewhere down the line, I finally did decide to plan my wedding. But since we were getting married, I also thought it was time to do the grown-up thing and buy a house.

I actually wasn't sure I'd be able to get a home loan and come up with enough for a down payment. But it all happened in the right way and at the right time. We found an old, cottage-style home in Selby.

It had me at hello.

I've never seen a house like it. And once I was done with it, it was a masterpiece. Well…it was my masterpiece, anyway! I did pretty much everything, new floors, carpets, all new paint, new windows, backsplash, laundry, painted the garage in our backyard RED like a barn because it was shaped like a barn. It was something I loved very much.

I spent a ton of money renovating the house. And I loved every minute of it.

And for a last-minute wedding that I threw together in a few months, my Wedding #2 was very nice too. This time, we got married in a beautiful Lutheran church—my very Christian grandmother had insisted on a church wedding this time, and I agreed. My entire family was there to see me walk down the aisle again. Justin's mother made my wedding dress, which was really meaningful, and his dad let us take out his Road Runner (his precious, restored baby he rarely let people drive) right after the wedding. So we zoomed off into the sunset with this beautiful black and white custom car.

It was romantic and actually kind of exciting. Even though, just like with my first wedding, there was no honeymoon. Just a return to the real world.

I remember a conversation I had with my mom right before I was going to get married. Once again, she was asking those pesky questions like she did with Bart. "Are you sure you're ready for this? Are you sure he's the one?"

I could tell my mom knew something wasn't right. She wouldn't have questioned it otherwise. And at that moment, right before I was about to walk down the aisle, I knew deep down inside that I was giving up. I was giving up on myself and just accepting this life that was unfolding in front of me.

Of course I had dreamed of something different. But Justin happened, and Justin wasn't a dream, he was a real, flesh and blood man—and a good one. I'd be silly not to marry him, right?

But on some level, I knew...

As it turned out, being married to Justin wasn't all that different than living with Justin. Mostly, my day-to-day life was still about my work.

Up until I started in sales, the only way for me to move ahead had been to ask for it. No one at One World ever came to me with any interest in what I could do for them. No one spotted my potential and said, "Hey, this would be great for Chelsea."

I had to be the one to see the need, to think of how to fill it, to propose it to management, and then, of course, to do a great job at it.

And still, they didn't even seem to notice that I was doing well!

But that all changed when I started doing sales. Suddenly, people were like, "Wow, she really is good at this." I guess they kind of had to notice, because no one in the history of the company had ever sold as much as I did that fast. And of course, sales is the thing that gets you noticed, because, more than anything else, sales is the thing that makes the company money.

So what started as a part-time, "Let's see how I can help" kind of thing turned into a full-time position pretty quickly. At the same time, I kept working on business development, because I had learned so much about One World in my three or so years there, I had tons of ideas on how they could grow the business more. There were things we could do with package branding, with up-leveling our service, so many opportunities to make One World an even stronger company.

I had finally reached the point where I had the courage to say, I am worth more. I knew that my on-the-job experience was finally enough to take me somewhere else, that my lack of formal education no longer mattered, that I was ready for a big career. And One World responded. They gave me a title—Director of Sales and Business Development. I reported directly to the VP. And I finally got put on salary instead of making an hourly wage, which was a huge thing.

Justin was really excited about my success too. And why not? I was making more money. I was always the breadwinner in my marriage—I paid the bills, paid for everything really.

But then something happened that Justin didn't like so much.

I got the opportunity to travel.

One World started sending me to trade shows. I went to Portland and then LA, and I absolutely loved it. Okay, I didn't love the trade show part itself. Sitting in a booth in some convention center all day long was not the most fun. But I met some great people and had some great conversations—conversations that didn't happen so often in Mobridge, South Dakota. I met people that actually owned their own businesses. They were crushing it in sales, like I was, but they were doing it for themselves, building their own futures instead of somebody else's.

And I started thinking, gosh, I wish that were me. And then…

…wait a minute. It could be me!

I learned the entire business at One World, pretty much top to bottom, in just three years. I could run that operation—so why couldn't I run my own?

It was a pretty exciting realization. But Justin could not understand why on earth I would want to do this. First of all, he hated it when I traveled. He basically hated travel, period. He was the kind of guy that grew up in Selby, graduated high school, stayed there and worked on his dad's ranch and didn't really want much more from life.

The idea of me looking for something outside of One World, maybe even outside of Mobridge, that might take me away and have me traveling, was something he just couldn't comprehend.

And suddenly, I found myself in this really hard place. Was this all life held for me at 23—to keep working hard at One World but not go anywhere, just do what I was doing for the rest of my life? To be the breadwinner, to have a family, then to have to take care of my family...

Suddenly, I felt like, how did I get here? That version of the future didn't sound like very much fun at all.

I found myself bored and daydreaming—curious about other things in life. It just felt like there was more out there. There had to be. And I wanted it.

Then I went to San Diego.

THE BIG IDEA

It was just another trade show—I went with Stewart, the VP who believed in me and taught me all the technical stuff. What made this trip different was the hotel. The event was held at this beautiful, swanky hotel called the Hotel Solamar. It was just incredible, the most amazing hotel I'd ever seen in my life, full of color and great design. And One World put me up there—the room was like $400 a night.

It was like nothing I'd ever experienced before. For example, there was room service! Here I was in this gorgeous, incredible hotel room eating good food *that someone brought to my door just because I called and asked for it!*

I felt so grown up.

I remember sitting in that hotel room so clearly—the comforter was chocolate brown with white polka dots. It was like the coolest bed ever. And it was just really inspiring, being around all this beautiful stuff. I realized that this was what I wanted from my life. I wanted a career that would let me travel and meet new people and stay in beautiful places.

But how could I get it?

I had built a great career for myself at One World—I had started at the bottom and worked my way up in just a few years. But the reality was, I'd gone about as high as I could possibly go. The only other place for me would be taking the job of the CEO's wife (VP of Sales)—or the CEO.

And obviously that wasn't going to happen.

So, sitting there in my stylin' room with my polka dots and room service, I stayed up all night brainstorming ideas for a business—my own business that I could create and grow on my own, that would give me the kind of life that I dreamed about. I didn't really know what I'd offer at that point, but I had learned so much in the last three years at

One World, I felt like I really could do just about anything anyone asked of me. So I just decided I'd call it marketing.

After all, when you get right down to it, everything is marketing.

The next day, sitting on the plane back to South Dakota, I told Stewart that I wanted to start a business. And Stewart, that amazing man who believed in me, was there for me again.

He actually took me seriously.

He asked me a bunch of really great questions that helped me think about what I could offer to people and how. And when I told him how the thing that inspired me was the hotel—that the beautiful hotel was the reason I stayed up all night and came up with this crazy plan—he suggested I call my business Solamar Marketing.

It was perfect.

I didn't know exactly what I was going to do or how I was going to do it. But I had a name and an idea. Nothing was going to stop me now.

CHAPTER 7

BECOMING A BUSINESSWOMAN

 Sometimes following your heart
means losing your mind.

—UNKNOWN

I got back from San Diego just bursting with ideas for my new business. I knew I needed to focus on the things I was good at—serving customers and coming up with solutions for them.

Of course, I told my husband what my super-exciting new plan was. He wasn't thrilled. Beyond that, he just didn't understand what was going on in my brain. In his mind, work was just about having enough money to pay for what you needed—not something that was supposed to be challenging, or exciting, or fulfilling. Work was just... work.

So I gave up and just stopped talking about it. But that didn't mean I wasn't going to do it.

I was committed.

I thought about how hard it was to start a business and get clients. Like, where the hell was I supposed to start and not do pro bono work? I realized that my computer skills were probably the best thing I could offer.

Obviously, if I was going to have a business, I needed a website. So I found one of those "done-for-you" website systems, found the template that looked the most like me, filled in the blanks and, voila! Solamar Marketing was on the internet! I was on my way! Okay, it wasn't the prettiest or most professional-looking website on the web, but it was up, it was mine, and it meant that Solamar was officially open for business.

I started doing logo/brand work for friends and family right away. The jobs were mostly collateral material design, branding and logos. I did it all myself too. I started designing using Microsoft Word—which I realize is very unsophisticated, but at the time, it was all I knew! Eventually I taught myself Photoshop, and even a little bit of InDesign. It wasn't like I was making big bucks—it was more a side gig to add some extra income and allow me to be creative.

And at that point, I only saw Solamar as a side thing. I had no idea how I could possibly do what I was doing full-time. Although I wanted to and I dreamed about it, I just thought it was out of reach. I built my company, I branded it before it even existed, but I really had no idea what it would become.

And neither did anyone else.

That's not because I kept my new venture a secret. My coworkers at One World knew all about Solamar and how excited I was. And like most things I started (except for sales, where there was just no denying me!), it was just another cute little example of curious Chelsea trying stuff. I would talk about it a little bit, and everyone would look at me like, "Yeah, right."

I don't think any of them took it seriously that I was trying to do this thing on my own. No one asked or cared or anything like that—except for Stewart. He was always in my corner, always cheering me on.

And I have to admit that even then, the wheels in my brain were turning. The one thing that I always hoped for was a way to work with people and love what I did. When I was initially starting to think about building the business, my dream was just to be able to pay my bills. My thought process was basically, "If I could get one client or two clients that I could actually support somehow—marketing, customer service or whatever—and make enough to live doing it, then I could quit my job."

All I wanted was to make enough money to pay my bills and to actually live. That's all I cared about. I didn't have this big vision of building a big business; I didn't have this sense of "I know where I'm going," I just knew that in that moment, I wanted to find something more impactful in my life than a situation where I felt like I was a tool and being used by people.

And despite my success at One World, I did feel a little like a tool.

Especially knowing how much business I was bringing in for that company—I can't even fathom how much money I made for them. Still, with everything I had accomplished in just a few years, I had already climbed as far as I could possibly climb on One World's corporate ladder. For a 24-year-old—or at least a curious 24-year-old—that just wasn't enough. I wanted more from life.

BRINGING UP MY BABY

My husband thought that the "more" that I wanted from life should follow a more traditional path. That meant starting a family. I always wanted to have kids—it was always my intention to have a family. But, like our wedding before, I kept finding reasons to put this new life change off. I didn't feel ready, and I certainly didn't hear my biological clock ticking.

There was a different baby I needed to nurture along. And I have to admit, those baby steps were amazing.

My first big moment was when I designed a logo for a friend that was opening a clothing boutique. She got this giant sticker sign/decal on her window made from the logo I created for her. It was amazing to see my work in a shop window and know that I did it, that it was mine.

I was so proud.

Eventually, I decided if I really wanted to go for it, if I wanted Solamar to be more than just a side business, I needed to treat it like something more than a side business.

Well, at the time it was more like, "I need a logo!" "I need a website!"

That's when I found Jill.

All the things I needed to do to grow the business were on my mind 24/7. But I didn't have any extra money because I was still living paycheck-to-paycheck. Yes, even though I was the Director of Sales and Business Development, reporting directly to the VP, I wasn't making enough money to pay for a website and logo.

Pretty sad, right? I know when you make more money, you spend more money, too. But there isn't really that much to spend money on in South Dakota. The reality was, I wasn't getting paid a whole lot at One World. Especially considering what I was delivering for them. Which made getting my own business off the ground that much more important.

So I did what any just-starting-out entrepreneur does.

I got a credit card.

Then I used my new card to hire this woman named Jill to design a professional website and logo for me. I think I spent like $1500 or something. It was probably the best investment I ever made.

Especially because Jill is still with me today.

Next, I worked on a business plan for Solamar. And I realized that since I was in a tiny town in South Dakota (and still working a full-time, corporate job), I needed a way to reach out to the wider world for clients without letting the One World team know that I was actively looking for "something else."

Even though I don't think anyone ever thought I would actually leave One World. That was just, like, not possible in anyone's mind.

Except mine.

My solution was LinkedIn. I put some serious work into beefing up my profile, showcasing what I had done for One World, the skills I had developed and the new projects I was doing with Solamar.

And before long, my profile caught the attention of a headhunter.

She told me she had a client who was looking for a project manager, and that I could do the work entirely over the internet. Of course, I had never been a satellite project manager before—my work had been solely for bricks and mortar businesses. But then again, if not me, who? I knew I was organized. I knew I could manage.

And I knew more than anything that what I wanted most in the world was to grow my own business and get out of my corporate job.

So I told the headhunter everything she wanted to hear. I said I could do a lot of things that I had no idea about doing. Seriously. There were points when I had no idea what she was talking about! But no matter how clueless I felt inside, I acted like I not only knew how to do everything, but that I was a pro at it all. I felt like this was my one shot—it was what I had to do to get my foot in the door.

Was I scared? A little. But after my years at One World, if there was one thing I knew about myself it's that I learn on the job—fast. And that I will dedicate myself 150% to making something work. Okay, that's two things.

But the bottom line was, I just told her I knew how to do everything her client needed.

I applied. I went through a series of interviews.

And I got the job.

MY FIRST BIG CLIENT

I was hired to manage the Personal Family Lawyer Program for a woman named Alexis Neely who had a company called FWPI—Family Wealth Planning Institute.

And that project—well, it was more than a project, it was a job—totally changed my life. Especially since, instead of working for Alexis, I was able to run the project entirely through Solamar.

So I wasn't just working for her company. I was finally working for my own.

The job was 100% virtual—my very first introduction to the virtual world. Before that, I had no idea it existed. I remember telling my grandma, "I got this job, it's online, it's for this person, I'm the project manager…"

Her response?

"You're not doing anything illegal, are you?"

It wasn't illegal, but since I was still working at One World, it was definitely on the down low. At first, it was basically part-time hours—so I didn't *necessarily* tell either of my "bosses" that I was working both jobs at the same time.

So I worked at One World during the day and on Solamar at night. Night and day—no joke. And I loved every minute of it.

I felt so alive and real when I worked. When I didn't work, I wasn't happy with my life. I just really dug myself into my work and it kind of defined me. It felt like that was all I had.

On the other hand, Justin thought I was totally ridiculous. He was always upset that I was spending so much time working and not hanging out with him. I tried to explain that I was building something bigger than me. Something I could be proud of and work hard for and build from.

But the more I explained, the more he didn't understand.

Then again, not many people did understand. Of course, again, no one took me seriously. When I talked about the virtual stuff, they thought I was lying. Or like I was talking some crazy science fiction stuff or something. There were (and still are) a lot of people out there—especially in small town South Dakota, but in plenty of other places too—that didn't know this kind of thing was possible. So at first, I just got a lot of flak for it.

No one looked at me like I was making something of myself.

But I knew something amazing was happening. Going virtual with Alexis' company, I learned so much. It was just insane and it was addicting. It was like Pop Rocks exploding in my brain—being introduced to this totally infinite world of possibilities that I had known absolutely nothing about.

My project was managing a virtual program Alexis provided to a group of lawyers. It was a year-long program that provided them with tools and resources to market their businesses. This is where I really started to understand marketing in a much bigger way. I reported to a woman named Laura Lee, who was (and still is!) the most patient person I knew. She mentored me and taught me everything—which, it turned out, was quite a lot. Remember, I claimed to know a lot more than I actually did when I applied for this job!

Working under Laura Lee, I learned not only how to work virtually, but also about programs and products that I didn't really understand that can be sold online. I saw how Alexis supported like 60 lawyers in her program—all online—by providing them the resources and the tools and coaching to build successful firms. And this wasn't her only program. She was incredibly successful at this point; she was probably a million-dollar online business.

I was so on fire with the possibilities—so hungry for more, Laura Lee saw that spark in me and realized that I was ready to grow with FWPI and do great work. After a month, she offered me a full-time position—making as much money as I was making at One World! That meant my dream was actually coming true. I could quit my "day job" and devote all my time to Solamar. It was the break I had been waiting for.

I was 24 years old, and my life was about to happen.

But Justin was not quite as excited as I was. The way he saw it, I was the breadwinner, the person who paid the mortgage, the person who carried our health insurance and handled everything financial in our lives. He thought I was crazy to leave a stable, corporate job working for a "real" company for what was basically the same amount of money, minus the benefits, to work for myself. He didn't see it as the beginning of something bigger—he only saw it as something scary...and a little nuts.

I tried explaining to him—I really wanted to do something with myself, I was only 24, I wasn't done yet. I wanted to go places, I wanted to see things, I wanted to marvel at things, I wanted to see the world.

So I gave notice at One World.

It did not go over well.

MOVING ON

What screws us up most in life is the picture in our head of how it is supposed to be.

—SOCRATES (ROUGHLY TRANSLATED!)

I tried to be as decent and supportive of the company as I could. I appreciated all One World had done for me, so when I gave notice to Stewart, I gave them a whole month to work out how they would replace me. Well, Stewart was fine, and supportive, and generally awesome as always.

But the CEO, who lived in California, was just furious. He called me on the phone and proceeded to chew me out, calling me every word under the sun (none of which I will print here!). He was so mad at me. Looking back, I understand why he was so upset. I was bringing in a lot of money, I did a lot for the company, and I don't think anyone ever thought I would ever leave.

But while I was—and am—eternally grateful to him and everyone at One World for the opportunity they gave me and for everything I learned there, and loved the CEO and his family dearly, it was time to move on. I was in love with the idea of having my own business, of controlling my own destiny and doing it on my own.

And now, I finally had my shot.

But in order to make this new beginning, there needed to be another ending.

I always wondered if my life would have been different if I was just strong enough to have realized that although Justin was a great guy, he just wasn't the right guy for me. But through all of our misunderstandings and miscommunications and basically living on different planets, I continued to believe that there was something I could do to make the situation better. My mom always told me to make the best out of everything, to play the cards I was dealt. So I just kept plugging through, thinking, I can do this, I can be happy.

But I don't think I ever was.

I loved Justin. Truly did love him. But it didn't make me happy.

I tried to talk with him about how we wanted different things from life, and that the things he wanted weren't working for me. But we couldn't really have conversations about it because he just didn't understand. It was a frustrating thing, so I just stopped talking about it. Anytime I would, it would be painful.

He just didn't get it.

Soon after I left One World, I told him I needed to spend some time away. I packed up a few things and went to stay with my sister in North Dakota—after all, now that I was working virtually, I could live and work anywhere.

Justin would come up and we'd try to talk—but no matter how much he wanted me to, I just couldn't go back to the life we had. I loved him, but I couldn't live with him—not the way he wanted to live. It was really sad. Really hard. We both cried. He was just broken—and I broke him. I broke us.

He would have stayed with me forever.

But I just couldn't do it anymore.

Finally, I told him we needed more time to be away from each other—and that eventually became permanent.

I wanted to get away so badly I told him to keep everything. Including the house that we bought.

I didn't want him to have to adjust his life because of my decision. I wanted him to stay in the house and keep all my things so he wouldn't have to go through the additional pain of rebuilding with new stuff. I loved that house, I loved fixing it up, I loved decorating it and creating a home. But it wasn't the right home for me. It wasn't ultimately a home where I could be happy.

So I just took a few very important things of mine. I packed what I could fit in my Toyota Camry and that's all I took with me. I never looked back.

And it was the most freeing thing I've ever done.

To this day, I think about Justin and hope he's happy and doing well. And that he'll find it in his heart to forgive me someday.

But I still carry this burden around. I failed him, and I hurt his life.

That's something I never wanted to do.

CHAPTER 8

CONFESSIONS OF A WORKAHOLIC

 Stay close to anything that makes you glad you are alive.

—HAFIZ

Okay, now that the last sad part of the book is out of the way—I promise!—let's backtrack a tiny bit… back to my first day of work after I left One World.

I woke up really early that morning with one prevailing thought in my head:

"Holy shit…is this a dream?"

Once I was conscious enough to realize that no, it was not a dream, and, yes, I did not have to drive to One World that day (or ever again), I knew it was time to get down to business.

It was totally and completely crucial that I did well. Not that it wasn't crucial before, but now it was crucial-er, because I had nothing to fall back on. There was no more corporation behind me to catch me. I was all by my lonesome. And I couldn't help feeling like—at any given time --something could happen that would take it all away.

It felt too good to be true. To be honest, it still does today. Like, pinch me, pinch me...someone?!!!

So my first step was getting up really, really early that first day to make sure it was clear to everyone that I was a go-getter and was there to prove myself. Not that any of the people I was out to impress were actually awake at the time to witness my commitment to early rising, hard work and overall excellence, but still! I was also SO happy that I was working at home—I didn't have to get dressed, put on makeup, do anything other than work, work, work. So I made myself some coffee to add even more fuel to the fire and got down to business.

First, I needed an "office." So I set up my computer, put a pen and paper next to it so I could take notes, made sure the phone was close by to talk with anyone who might need to hear my voice (or, more likely, answer my questions), and of course made room for the aforementioned coffee.

I was ready, people!

But, truth be told, I was also SUPER scared. As great as it was basking in the "nothing this awesome has ever happened to me before in my entire life" feeling, as I already mentioned, the "how can this possibly last?" feeling was following close behind. I mean, seriously?

Could I actually have built a real, live business out of thin air? Do people really do things like that?

Here's where my mindset pretty much saved my bacon. My attitude toward new things had always been (and still remains) I will MAKE this work. Whatever I need to do, I will make it work. I will do anything to make it work.

It was my mantra every day. Seriously.

And there was a lot to make work, because I was doing it all myself. Everything. Even the stuff I had absolutely no idea about—which is where Laura Lee came to my rescue again and again (and why I put that phone right there next to my computer and my coffee). But even where I might have been clueless or confused, I also had this great, deep love for the work I was doing and excitement about doing it myself—not to mention the fact that I was on fire about the future I was creating. I had been in this position before, with bookkeeping, with account managing, with selling. So I just figured it out and delivered.

And I did really, really well.

And of course, lived happily ever after.

Sort of.

ALL WORK & NO PLAY...

Because, as you might have guessed, there was a dark side to this cloud of happy self-sufficiency. What also tends to happen when you do everything yourself, and there are a whole lot of those things to do, is you get burned out. And I pretty much got *fried*. I was working 15-hour days, which left me about 9 hours to sleep, eat, shower and have a life (like that was gonna happen!). So there were a few times where I felt pretty close to the breaking point.

That's when I remembered Jill.

Jill had done amazing work on the Solamar website—much better than anything I could have pulled together on my own. But I felt nervous and unsure about paying another person to do the work I was contracted to do for my client. Not that she wouldn't be amazing—I had no question about that. The big question was, could I afford to bring someone else on? Would that be irresponsible, or too risky, or wrong for some reason that didn't occur to me?

Whatever might have been going through my mind, Jill's greatness turned out to be a much more powerful force.

I don't remember exactly how it hit me—probably when I was in the middle of a design project that was way above my skill level—but I suddenly realized, "Hey! Jill could do this!" Followed closely by, "Hey! I could also offer some seriously amazing design work through Solamar if I contracted with Jill!"

So I did.

I guaranteed her a certain number of hours per month and I basically became her pimp—selling her work and allowing Solamar to provide an extra level of service and expertise to our clients.

That was really what it was all about—working hard and doing my best. But I didn't have a "mission statement" or overreaching company philosophy at the time. I was so busy working and growing my business to ensure its survival, what my business stood for was probably the last thing I thought about.

Of course, it was always there, hidden in some corner of the back of my mind. I just didn't have time to articulate it. I barely had time to breathe!

But at the end of the day, I guess I always did have an underlying philosophy. And it was pretty much the same thing it has always been—to do my best and to deliver for my clients (and later, my team). To ensure that everyone feels taken care of and heard. I put myself last. That's how Solamar became successful. It was really just basic customer service.

Take care of your clients and your staff—and you'll have a successful business. That's the definition of success.

Outside of work (as if I had a life outside of work), I was ready to get on with things—primarily finding a place to live. I had left a house that I had loved, filled with things I loved, and had been living with my sister. But because things were going so well, it wasn't long before I felt ready to head out on my own again.

I found a really incredible condo that I loved. Yes, it was pricey. But I was a businesswoman—an entrepreneur—and a successful one at that! I was in a place where I could afford it, so I snagged it and made it great and loved it even more…

…for about six months.

That was about how long it took for my old friend curiosity to pop its head back into my life.

Because eventually, I got past the hard part of launching Solamar full-time and figured stuff out. So then I was in North Dakota, in a great condo—running my successful company—and I felt bored! Even though I was still working at least 10 hours a day. But that old dream of getting out of states with Dakota in their name and getting out into the world of brighter lights and bigger cities kept gnawing at me.

In those few minutes a day I wasn't working or sleeping.

TRAVELS WITH CHELSEA

Luckily, the folks at FWPI were more than willing to give me things to do that accommodated my wanderlust. I started traveling pretty frequently. Since they were located in L.A., I went out to California a lot, which definitely didn't suck. Going to L.A. on a regular basis just seemed like some crazy dream on some level to a girl from small town North Dakota—now I was regularly flying into LAX—so often that the security people recognized me!

Plus I took trips to manage the company's lawyer retreats in Cape Cod, Atlanta and Florida. And I was still so young—only 24 years old.

Which brings up kind of a funny story…

When I flew into Atlanta on one of my FWPI trips, management wanted me to rent a car. Something I had never done before. But I'd done lots of things I'd never done before in the past year…how hard could it be?

Still, I was super-nervous filling out the paperwork. If you've ever rented a car, you know what I mean. It's all so official, like you're assuming responsibility for this very expensive…thing.

And when they asked to see my driver's license, and I showed them, it turned out I had even more of a reason to be nervous.

They rejected me!

Turns out they don't rent cars to people under 25. Who knew?

I mean, seriously, I didn't feel 24. I'd been running a business, working my butt off for years, taking care of myself, not to mention the fact that I had two marriages and divorces under my belt. I felt more like I was 44.

Still, little glitches like being too young for car renting aside, it was so much fun. I got to live that dream I had when One World put me up at the Hotel Solamar in San Diego and I brainstormed my business in the first place. But now, I was living that dream over and over again—and I was seeing some of the coolest places in the country. Cape Cod was definitely the dreamiest, most beautiful place I got to visit. The resort where I stayed was just insane. I was at another incredible resort in Florida where I tried sushi for the very first time—not a lot of raw fish on the menu in small Dakota towns (unless the cook really messes up). A team member made me try it, and I was absolutely terrified at the idea of putting a raw fish in my mouth…and then swallowing it…ewwwwww.

But guess what? Sushi is now my favorite food.

And when I couldn't travel for my job, I found reasons to travel just for me. I went to New York City, Chicago and Salt Lake City just because I wanted to, because I wanted to visit those places I'd only heard about or seen in pictures or on TV and experience them first hand. After all, there was nothing stopping me. Working remotely, I could have set up my office on a mountaintop in the Himalayas, if I wanted to. It was a huge growth experience for me—a little lonely and scary at times, but always challenging and inspiring.

And honestly, I had the best of both worlds. Wherever I went all by myself, when I was done traveling, I got to come home to North Dakota and be close to my family. Which was part of what I needed to finally build the kind of stable life and foundation I wanted after all the drama of my first 24 years.

The bottom line was, in my work, my travels and my time alone, I was finally finding myself. I know that might sound cheesy, but I was definitely the type of person that could have easily ended up trying to squeeze herself into someone else's life—as in a man's life. After all, I had tried that with Justin, and the results were kind of a disaster. But now, for the first time ever, I was living on my own, supporting myself, working hard and feeling like I was actually making a difference in the world.

And yes, as corny as it sounds, I was getting to know *me*.

Yes, I'm fully aware of the cheese factor of that statement. But this was seriously the first time in my whole life I stopped for two seconds to find out how I like MY eggs, what are MY favorite colors, what are MY favorite hobbies. It finally had nothing else to do with anyone else's preferences or ways or ideas.

It was just me.

Well, me and my business. Which was an extension of me.

And if you know me, you know…I'm always looking for the next thing, the next experience.

Despite all the work and the travel, I was still feeling a little restless in North Dakota. When I was home, sometimes I felt bored. It was a good, stable thing for me to be there and be close to family, no doubt. But I wanted more. I couldn't help it. It's just my nature.

So I packed up all my things again—and moved to Santa Rosa Beach, Florida. I did know one person there, my guide and friend Laura Lee, so I wouldn't be totally alone. Still, my parents were not exactly psyched about this decision. In fact, I remember their reaction being more like, "What the hell?"

But I was able to rent a beach house (and afford it). I did know that ONE person…so I figured that would count for something. And I could work from wherever I wanted to work, so why not? I wanted to experience something different.

I also wanted my business to grow. At some point along the line, I realized that the only way to continue to build Solamar would be to expand beyond working primarily and exclusively for one client. So I took another risk and let Alexis know that I really wanted to grow my own business—and that the only way to do it was to pull back a little on my work with FWPI.

If you're an entrepreneur, you've no doubt heard some version of the saying, "don't just work IN your business, work ON your business." Well, I know for a fact that it's true. I was spending so much time working in someone else's business, I was doing an awesome job of building that business, but kind of neglecting my own. So FWPI ultimately became a smaller client, with Solamar just handling some design work and some membership stuff.

And I was able to shift my focus to getting and servicing additional clients. That's really when Solamar began to become the company it is today.

GROWING MY BUSINESS

Most of the time, my clients would find me by word of mouth. Someone would hear about Solamar or my work from a friend or a colleague and they'd be interested in learning more about what I did. I also started doing some email marketing and some social media marketing to reach out beyond that circle of "people who knew people I knew."

My ultimate goal was to get someone—anyone—on the phone. Once that happened, I knew I could sell them what we had to offer. And no, it's not that I was arrogant or anything, only that I was so confident in our services and what we could do for our clients.

Okay, and after the time I spent selling at One World, I definitely had plenty of confidence in that whole sales thing…

So slowly but surely, the clients kept coming in. At the beginning, Solamar primarily focused on design and project management. That was really the nuts and bolts of what people wanted at the time—and really all we did. And before long, it was enough to keep us growing beyond the point where I could handle the majority of the work myself, even with the smaller workload from FWPI.

That meant I needed people. People who shared my philosophy and wanted to be a part of my dream. So I started hiring Account Managers to take over some of the work I had done managing projects for clients. I looked for people with the same passion that I had, with a background in administration, or customer service, or project management. I brought on people who knew about online marketing and how to do it successfully. And of course we had Jill, our amazing designer, working with all of our clients to provide design wherever it was needed.

Suddenly, I was managing a pretty awesome team.

Of course, for some reason, I was still working at least 10 hours a day. But that was more about me than them…

You have to find what sparks a
light in you so that you, in your own
way, can illuminate the world.

–OPRAH WINFREY

Around this point, a philosophy of sorts finally started to emerge for me. I call it Working on Purpose.

What exactly do I mean by that? Let me explain...

After everything I've done in my life, I really think anyone can create a business and make money. It's not rocket science. After all, I am clearly not a rocket scientist...

But if you're not doing work on purpose—and really making an impact in the world for the greater good—then why are you doing it? For me, having a business means that every day I have an opportunity to take care of people. I want to take care of my staff, my clients—and help them make their dreams of running their own successful businesses or careers come true.

We did that then. And we still do that today. Every day.

Of course, working on purpose was one thing. Living on purpose was still somewhere off in the future for me.

Because at this point, the purpose of my life was basically one thing and one thing only—to work.

After two failed marriages, I vowed that I was through with love. It wasn't something I missed all that much. I felt okay with being on my own and being alone. I enjoyed it. So I didn't date anyone for about a year—I had no interest in being in a relationship, dating, or even really being social outside of work. I was interested in being a wanderer, a gypsy. I wanted to drink life in.

Except sometimes, drinking alone can get a little lonely.

Part 3

SPREADING
MY WINGS

CHAPTER 9

LIVING ON
PURPOSE

When I saw you I fell in love, and
you smiled because you knew.

— SHAKESPEARE

So there I was, in a beautiful Florida beach town, all by
my lonesome. Well, I had Laura Lee, but she had a life
of her own.

I didn't.

I was living in one of the most beautiful places I'd ever
been, but it's not like I was enjoying it. I hadn't really made
any new friends—mainly because I still worked constantly,
and barely ever got out of my house to experience all the
stuff I'd supposedly moved to Florida for!

So one typically perfect, sunny Saturday (aren't they
all in Florida?), I called my mom and told her that was it, I
was ready to come home. I was lonely, I missed my family—
and I just missed small town North Dakota. Florida was

great, but it was full of "snowbirds" and seasonal renters—not the kind of people I could build a new life with.

My mom listened to me. She really wanted me home too. But instead of asking what time my flight was getting in, she said,

"Chelsea, you are going to take a shower, shave your legs, put something cute on—and take yourself out to lunch today."

My response? "You're ridiculous. I'm not going out to eat by myself!"

Plus I had no interest in showering that weekend. Ha!

Then my mom—bless her heart—hung up on me! She was that serious. After everything she'd seen me take responsibility for and deal with in my 25 years, she couldn't deal with me being in this place where I was lonely and feeling sorry for myself.

She just wouldn't have it.

In fact, she was so serious that she called back about 20 minutes later to make sure I got in the shower. Of course I was still sitting there in my PJs, with no intention of doing anything (except work, of course). But, seeing as my mom cared enough to call back, I got in the shower, shaved my legs, threw on some summer clothes and headed out to find lunch.

It was about 2PM when I walked into a place called Bud and Alley's, a bar/grill/restaurant that's set in this

gorgeous, perfect spot right on the Gulf of Mexico—
and like five minutes from my house. So it wasn't like it
required a major effort to get myself there. Although I still
felt a little ridiculous walking into a restaurant all alone.

It helped that the place was empty—other than one
other person at the bar.

I sat down, ordered a drink and sat there enjoying the
hot weather and the beautiful setting and the gazillion
TVs they had on. Of course, this was the South, it was late
summer, so every single one of those TV's was turned to a
different channel of football.

College football.

Now, I have absolutely no interest whatsoever in college
football. But I was so nervous being alone at this bar, I
decided I would act as if I was, in fact, hugely interested
in college football. I sipped my drink and watched, not
exactly sure of who I was watching, or what they were
doing, or who was winning.

Maybe because I was so not into football, maybe
because something about him just spoke to me, I couldn't
help glancing at the one other person in Bud and Alley's
that day—the guy who was sitting all alone on the other
side of the bar. He looked sad. He looked bored.

Kind of like me.

I just couldn't get over it. I felt so bad for him, sitting there eating alone. So I turned to him and asked, "Is anyone sitting next to you?"

He was a little shocked. He was like, "Ahhuuuuhhggmmmm…no…"

So I moved over and sat next to this stranger. And of course, given the intense interest in college football I had been working so hard to show, the first question out of his mouth was, "What team are you rooting for?"

Busted.

I remember thinking, "Oh shit, some guy living in the South is asking me about college football, which I know nothing about!"

So I said, "Uh…all of them?"

That's how I met the man who would eventually become my husband, as well as my partner and the love of my life, Mark Berler.

And, according to Mark at least, that was also the moment he fell in love with me.

See, even though Mark lived in the South (he had a house in Florida and primarily lived in Birmingham, Alabama), he was actually a New York City boy and not a college football fan at all. So my answer confirmed a couple of important things for him.

#1. I was not an insane college football fan, and,

#2. I was not even from the South!

He didn't tell me at the time, but later he told me that he was laughing on the inside at my answer to his question.

I, of course, had no idea any of this was going on inside Mark's head. In my mind, he was a guy sitting alone at a bar that maybe needed a friend. I wasn't thinking about dating anyone or having any type of relationship.

But after we finished our lunch, instead of saying goodbye and going on his way, Mark asked me if I've ever had a tour of 30A. 30A, for those of you who've never been to Northwest Florida, is the highway that runs along the Gulf Coast outside the town of Destin, which is where Santa Rosa Beach is located. It's like a little secret paradise.

I told him no, not really—I'd been working a lot and hadn't had a chance to explore the area (and was spending a lot of time in my jammies feeling sorry for myself. Okay, I left out that part.).

So he asked if he could take me for a ride around town. I, being the agreeable person that I am, of course said yes.

And then promptly thought to myself. "My mom is going to kill me. I'm leaving with some guy I don't know?? WHAT JUST HAPPENED???"

We walked down to where the cars were parked and, lo and behold, his car was actually a motorcycle. He was on a freakin' *chopper*. I was thinking, "Oh Jeez, now what have I gotten myself into?" But there was no graceful way to get out of it now. So I hopped on and let this strange man take me for a ride.

It was the best evening I've ever had.

The night was beautiful. Mark was such a gentleman. And riding on the back of that chopper, with the warm wind in my hair, was just exhilarating. Especially after spending the last few months cooped up in my house.

We drove around town on the chopper, ate dinner at Hard Rock Café in Destin, and later that evening, met up with some of his friends. At that point, he turned to me and asked, "Do you know how old I am?"

Which was kind of a strange question.

He looked about 35 or 36, which was older than me, but nothing scandalous or anything. So I said, "I don't really care" and shut that conversation down.

The truth is, I was already falling for him. I'd never met anyone who just swept me off my feet the way he did— who took charge and made it a point to show me a good time. I'd never felt so important and so cared for.

At the end of the evening, we exchanged phone numbers, but he was leaving for Birmingham, where he had a house, an ex-wife and two kids, the next day. I remember thinking, he has to go back home, I'll probably never see him again.

He said he'd call when he came back. And that he would, in fact, be back. I was like, "Yeah right…"

But he did call. He called a lot.

And he came back down to Florida that following weekend.

In fact, he came back even though he was really, really sick. He didn't want to cancel on me because he thought that if he stood me up, I would never really trust his whole, "I'll be back to visit" thing. So when he came back, I basically wound up taking care of him because he was too sick to go out and do anything.

Not that I minded.

I learned that he lived in Birmingham, but worked for a company out of Boston—he had moved to Birmingham when a previous job transferred him, and kept living in Alabama to be near his kids after he got divorced. He actually built a house right around the corner from his ex-wife, even though he is not exactly a Birmingham kind of person. You can take the man out of Manhattan, but you can't take the New York City out of the man!

He pretty much traveled for a living (and still does), working for a marketing agency like Solamar, only much bigger. His kids, Allison and Matt, were teenagers at the time—16 and 14. He told me he dedicated a lot of his weekends and time in the summer to them, to give them stability.

I was impressed that he was such a good dad.

MAD ABOUT MARK

I also found out that he was much older than I thought—not exactly surprising given the fact that he had two teenage kids.

Turns out he was (and is) 18 years older than me.

This was definitely a lot more than I expected. He didn't look 44—or at least not what I imagined 44 would look like. And I was already enjoying our time so much, I wouldn't have cared if he was 54!

But my mom cared. She cared a lot. When I told her about the awesome guy I'd been seeing—thanks to her brilliant advice to take a shower and shave my legs and get out of the house—she wasn't nearly as happy as I was.

In fact, she was not happy at all.

Given my history with men, I guess I shouldn't have been surprised that she wasn't exactly excited about me getting involved with a divorced man with two kids who was old enough to be my father—at least biologically.

But by this point, there was no stopping me. I was pretty much head over heels. I don't think Mark and I had even been hanging out for a month when we were driving and I was blabbering on about something and the words "I love you" somehow slipped out.

Oh crap! I couldn't believe I said that!

But Mark just paused and smiled. Then he said "What did you say?" and laughed.

And then he said, "I love you too."

I'd only known him a month, and we were already in love.

At that point, things started moving *really* quickly—as if the "I love you" in under 30 days wasn't fast enough. That meant talking about his kids. He told me he wanted to wait for me to meet them because he cared so much about them and about giving them stable lives. He wanted to be sure that we were serious, that we planned to stay together, before bringing me into their world.

But we didn't end up waiting very long.

About a month into our relationship we took a trip together, to Las Vegas for a weekend. We talked more about his kids, and he told me he was ready for me to meet them.

I was so excited.

The meeting was at the end of October. And it went so well that we ended up deciding to move in together right after Thanksgiving, which we were going to spend with his very cool, very New York family.

That was when we made the announcement.

It was kind of like, "Happy Thanksgiving. This is Chelsea. By the way, we're moving in together."

Luckily, by this point he had met my mom, and Bob, and the rest of my family, and they all fell in love with him (almost) as much as I did.

So I packed up and moved again, this time from Florida to Birmingham, so Mark and I could be together when he wasn't traveling. Of course, he still had the house in Florida, so we could still spend time there too.

Everyone thought we were both completely crazy because it happened so fast.

And then, almost as soon as things started to settle and that whirlwind died down, I met another person who would change my life almost as dramatically.

ANDREA

To be fully alive is not simply to drink
deeply of life and to be satisfied.
It's to become a well, offering
life to the world around you.

—JASON JAGGARD

Solamar was helping an event planner friend of mine with some work when a woman named Andrea Lee hired her to help with her event.

Yes, the same Andrea Lee who wrote the forward to this book. And who also changed my life.

From the first time I spoke to Andrea, I loved every minute I was lucky enough to be in contact with her. The way she communicated, what her voice sounded like—it just felt safe. Plus, unlike some clients, our relationship wasn't all about her.

When Andrea asks, "How are you," she actually listens to your answer.

I was so impressed with this Andrea person, I decided I never, ever wanted to stop working with her. So I reached out and asked if there was any way I could support her outside of the event—if she had any need for Solamar's services. She hired me to work on an affiliate marketing campaign, and our relationship just kept growing, until Solamar became her go-to team for almost everything.

Which basically turned Solamar into the company it is today.

I'd worked for a lot of really nice people, but Andrea was just incredible. Even before we met face-to-face, she became more than a client. She was my friend and my mentor. I knew I still had to impress her and make her feel taken care of, but she was so good to me that I wanted to work really, really hard for her—even by my crazy standards!

I never, ever wanted to let her down.

This commitment was tested the very first time I met Andrea face to face. I was running my first-ever event for her in San Francisco, and one member of my team, the AV guy, just completely sucked. Of course, I was trying to make it work, trying to cover for him, trying to fix it myself.

Then Andrea walked up to me and said, "You need to let him go."

I was floored. "Fire him? Me? You want me to do that?"

Her answer? "Yep."

I was dying.

I couldn't actually fire a person, could I? Then again, I wanted to do a good job for Andrea—I certainly wasn't going to let her down the first time I did an event for her! But, more than that, I knew that she had my best interests at heart. I knew that she was teaching me something through this whole unfortunate experience.

So I did it. Yes, I wanted to throw up, but I did it. And of course Andrea was right—it made the event awesome.

We still laugh about it to this day.

How and when to fire someone is just the tip of the iceberg when it comes to the things Andrea has taught me since we started working together. I don't even know where to start. Let's see—how to have conversations with people, how to serve them in the best possible way, how to listen, how to be an incredible leader.

But also, that there are more important things in life than work.

Yes, it took a client to teach me not to work so hard.

Also, some of my very closest friends are because of Andrea. Her husband, her brother, her General Manager— Jeremie. They are all family. And I'm so grateful Andrea brought us together.

Today, I'm a better leader, a better friend, a better wife, a better human being—all because I'm lucky enough to know Andrea. She was the first person in my crazy life outside of my family and Mark to really love all of me, not just because she wanted something, but to love the person I am in every way.

And, maybe because of that, she taught me how to finally love myself.

LOVE & MARRIAGE: THE FINAL CHAPTER

Meanwhile, Mark and I were having so much fun traveling and hanging out that despite the early "I love you's," the

"Will you marry me" took a little bit longer. Although we did, eventually, expand our family.

One Saturday, the kids and I talked Mark into taking a trip to the Humane Society. You know, just for "something to do."

We came home with two dogs. Not one, but two!

Initially, becoming a dog owner was not at all what Mark wanted. But now, Stella and Dakota (Kota for short) are his best friends too. Stella is crazy and hyper and nuts…and Kota is yummy, sweet, and full of love. When they wake me up in the morning they're the most fun, and they're the cutest when they're tired and just want to cuddle at night.

Of course, two dogs can also be a lot of work. But my life is better because of them. It's also fun to see Mark roll around with them when he's home…and how they keep us not so focused on work all the time. It makes us both appreciate the little things in life that play such an integral role in being happy.

However, just because we now had two "fur babies" didn't mean we were about to rush into anything more. Both of us being divorced, another marriage wasn't something either one of us thought we had to do right away.

But one day, after we'd been together about a year and a half, Mark took me to my favorite sushi restaurant with his kids. And right there, in front of the raw fish, he proposed to me.

I was completely surprised. I had no idea it was coming.

But my mom and Bob knew. Mark actually called them and asked for their permission—something that neither of my exes ever bothered with. And my family was thrilled to give that permission. After the initial freak-out over the age difference thing, they realized Mark is a pretty awesome guy. They loved that I was so happy. They'd never seen me that way before.

And they loved him for it.

Our wedding was just like heaven—like a wedding out of a book. It was on the beach, right in front of Bud and Alley's, the restaurant where I first sat down next to him at the bar. Which was sentimental and amazing, in addition to being just an awesome place to have a wedding. Allison stood up for me and Matt stood up for his dad—in addition to walking me down the aisle and "giving me away" to his dad. And all of our closest friends and family were there.

It was the best, most incredible day of my life.

But the day wasn't so awesome just because I got to have a wedding on the beach and party with all my friends and family at this amazing spot. It was because Mark and I were dedicating ourselves to each other and deepening our already incredible relationship. I had said wedding vows twice before, but this was the first time I *felt* them and believed what I was saying and doing with every inch of my heart and soul.

This time, I knew I was finally marrying the right guy.

Right after the reception, we went on our honeymoon—except it wasn't a typical honeymoon. We wanted to celebrate the family we'd become, so we went on a family-moon with Allison and Matt. The original plan had been to go somewhere overseas, but we weren't able to take the kids out of the country, so we went to San Francisco instead and had a great time just eating and playing together.

In my three marriages, it was my first honeymoon.

And I'm pretty sure it will be my last.

CHAPTER 10

MY LIFE SO FAR...

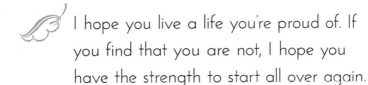 I hope you live a life you're proud of. If
you find that you are not, I hope you
have the strength to start all over again.

−F. SCOTT FITZGERALD

So here I am, not yet 30 years old, looking back on an incredibly eventful not-even-10 years. Two divorces. Three marriages. And a journey that has taken me from the curious girl no one really ever expected to amount to much of anything to the CEO of my own company.

My own successful company. I still can't believe it sometimes.

Solamar has grown so much that a few years ago, I made a decision I never thought I would make. I got an office. An actual office outside my house.

An office where I regularly see and interact with other human beings.

An office that I actually have to put clothes on to drive to.

Not that working from home isn't lovely. I still do it every week. But as Solamar grew, I realized I needed an outside space where I could have client meetings, or get together in person with my team, without having to make sure my house was clean.

So I made finding the perfect office a project—and it turned out to be a great project for me. First of all, Birmingham happens to be a super great city for young entrepreneurs. There's a really powerful energy and sense of community, and everyone is really supportive of each other. It was really, really exciting to become a part of that (even if I had to leave the house to do it).

Once I decided, yes, I was going to take the plunge, I drove around the city for a few days looking for the perfect home for Solamar. I saw a lot of decent spaces, but nothing that grabbed me. Then one day, I saw this space on the main road, about 15 minutes from home. And I swear, it spoke to me.

It said, "Hey, Chelsea! This is it!"

It was an office suite designed to look like the old warehouse buildings in downtown Birmingham, but completely, brand, spankin' new. Which made it the perfect funky, fun, creative space for me and my company.

I signed the lease the next day.

Once I had my space, my inner HGTV-watching, decorating maniac took over. I knew I wanted Solamar

World Headquarters (!) to have a specific look and feel. I wanted it to be as crazy and creative and free as possible. To me, that meant chalkboard walls that we could write ideas or inspirational notes or funny messages on. It meant fun prints and colors to inspire my team, and inspire me, and to just be a great, stimulating, welcoming place to come to work.

So, like my virtual business before, I built it.

As I write this, my office and I are in our third year together, and we're still madly in love. It's a fun place, a creative place, an inspiring place—just like I dreamed it would be.

I love it the most when the entire team is here. Regularly, there are just five of us who are based in Birmingham and come in every week. Which is awesome. But when the whole gang is here, when the energy is crackling and we're all together, it's so much fun. We've had up to 20 people in the place. Which is kind of like a party, except it's a party where work gets done.

Which, come to think of it, is probably *my* version of a party...

Our team of 20 now serves around 45 clients (in 5 different countries, too!). Which is pretty amazing considering Solamar has only been in existence in my *mind* since October, 2006, when I was a 22-year-old girl inspired by a really nice hotel room.

However.

YES, VIRGINIA, THERE IS A DOWN SIDE...

I don't want you to read this and think that it's all been perfect (from a business standpoint—you know the personal stuff hasn't!), and that everything's happened almost by magic. It's also been a lot of hard work, a lot of sleepless nights, a lot of wondering how I'm going to get through one tough experience or another. Of course, my childhood pretty much prepared me for anything.

But getting sued was still kind of a shocker...

Yes, I was actually sued. Me! One of the independent contractors I hired came after me saying I should have classified her as an employee instead of an independent contractor. That's the downside to virtual support and employing people across the United States—all state laws are different. Mark that down as GOOD TO KNOW!

Jeeshhh!

When am I supposed to learn all this legal stuff?

When am I supposed to sleep?

Attention all business owners out there...please have an attorney review all of your contracts!! <wink>

Anyway, she retained a lawyer—a lawyer she didn't even have to pay, because they were working on a contingency basis. Which means the lawyer was only going to get paid if I paid his client. So I was definitely going to have to pay, one way or another.

That's the thing about being sued. Even if the person suing you doesn't have a solid case against you, you still have to pay a lawyer to fight back! I figured out pretty fast that, even though I was being taken advantage of, it was in my best interest to settle pretty quickly and not let things drag on too long. That's my advice, in addition to the lawyer reviewing the contracts thing, should you ever get sued. Which I sincerely hope you don't.

But then again, getting sued also made me proud—in a twisted kind of way.

Because...I was finally worth suing! I was still in my 20's and I had a lawyer smelling dollar signs on me and coming after me. I remember thinking, "Yay, I've arrived! I can be sued because I have a real business!"

Maybe the fact that it happened right before Mark and I got married helped. I was in an especially positive mood. Even for me.

The fact that I was sued by an independent contractor brings me to the other really, really tough part of building Solamar, or any business. And that's the ebb and flow of building a team. I know I put a lot into people. Everyone I hire, I fall in love with. It's kind of like a little romance. But just like real-life romances, they don't always work out. Sometimes it's them. Sometimes it's you. Sometimes it's both of you.

But it does happen.

Luckily, we've had a solid core team for the last three or four years, which has been awesome. It gives me a great foundation to build from.

When I talk about building Solamar, what that really means to me is seeing how many families I can help. My dream isn't necessarily to be a bigger company, but to be a better company. And the thing I love most about it, the biggest perk of being a CEO, is that I can employ all of these people, take care of them, give them jobs and help them take care of their families.

Like my own family needed help so many years ago.

To me, that's the biggest gift of all. I love that we can truly help people make their dreams a reality, and make dreams a reality for our clients. How awesome is that?

It's the best of both worlds.

MRS. BERLER

Of course, the biggest change in my life—and the biggest joy—has been my marriage to Mark. After walking down the aisle two times for the wrong reasons, taking the plunge for a third time, with a guy who was 18 years older than me, might not have seemed like the most logical move.

But then again, since when has logic been a prerequisite for me?

Turns out my leap of faith has paid off. Since I've been with Mark, I find myself being so grateful and thankful for this life in the most incredible ways. I've never been so in love with someone.

Which is the way it's supposed to be, right?

I know, it sounds like I'm bragging, but I can't help it. I feel so lucky to be married to an incredible human being—a man who makes me want to be a better woman every day. I've learned so much from him. I'm a better person for knowing him. Sometimes there are no words to describe it.

Although I am doing my best here…

Mark is also a great dad, which has helped make being a stepmom an amazing, positive experience for me. I've seen enough fairy tales to know it doesn't always work out that way. But I love Allison and Matt so much—they're both such incredible, incredible kids. Mark and I spend every minute we possibly can with them, traveling with them, and of course, scarfing down lots and lots of sushi (the official food of the Berler Family) together. Of course, now that they're getting older and doing their own thing, I'm already experiencing a premature version of Empty Nest Syndrome.

I miss them coming around all the time the way they used to.

Mark does too.

But that's part of life. We grow, we change, and that's a good thing, not a bad thing. Matt is a senior in high school as I write this—he's an incredible athlete and just signed with a full ride to play baseball in Meridian, Mississippi. So he'll be off to college before I know it. Allison is already there. She's going to college at Mississippi State, where she's a cheerleader. She's also incredibly talented in art and photography. A girl after my own heart.

They're starting their own lives. And I couldn't be more excited for them.

Of course, as the kids move on with their own lives, Mark and I have our lives ahead of us, too. And eventually, that will hopefully mean moving to the beach house on 30A, back to the beautiful Florida town where Mark first swept me off my feet and onto the back of a chopper, full-time. For now, we still split our time between the house in Birmingham Mark built around the corner from his kids' mom and the beach house on 30A.

These days, we're not just close to the kids when we're at home in Birmingham. My mom and Bob are living there too. Which is pretty awesome for me. Bob put in for a transfer to the Home Depot here and he got it. So now we're in the same town, seeing each other all the time! Now—only if I could get my sisters to move!

And my parents absolutely love it in the South. After the cold of the Dakotas, it's a totally new thing for them.

Another great thing is, after so many years of struggle, their financial lives have finally gotten easier. Of course, they don't really spend any money—I think Bob would rather walk the streets of Birmingham in a frilly pink tutu than spend money!—but they're comfortable, they have what they need and they're happy. And of course, Mark and I love treating them to special surprises and showing them things they've never seen before.

Being able to do that is the best gift ever.

My sisters are still up in North Dakota. Alicia is in love—thanks (at least in part) to me! I connected with an old friend of hers, set them up, and the rest was history. She has two girls, Kambree and Avaree, who are super fun, into sports and just as goofy as ever. I love being an aunt. Almost as much as I loved playing matchmaker.

Jessica and her husband have been together since serving in Iraq. They were in two different companies for the National Guard—met and found out they were both from North Dakota, and have been inseparable ever since. They have two kids. Reed and Lola. The cutest things ever. They're so much fun to spend time with...and spoil rotten!

As for me…

I'm curious about becoming a mom. But not quite sure yet.

Right now, my priority is spending more time with my husband. We work a lot—he travels during the week—so we love our time together, and we'd really love to be together more. I've cut down on my traveling a lot, partially because I don't like leaving the dogs behind (I told you two dogs can be a lot of work!) Now, I only hit the road for Solamar once a month or so, so when Mark is home, I'm usually here.

Of course, traveling *with* Mark—meaning traveling for fun—is different. We check out a new exotic place, usually someplace warm and sunny, a few times a year. So far, my passport stamps include Curacao, St Kitts, the Bahamas, Aruba, the Dominican Republic, Costa Rica and Panama—all places in Central America and the Caribbean—plus we've been pretty much everywhere you can go in the USA. We're going all the way to South America, to Brazil next year, and I cannot wait.

Could I have kids and still do all that? Maybe not.

Still, some days I'd love to experience that connection with a child and with my husband that I've seen my sisters experience. But there are other days when I feel like the world is too overpopulated and I'm not sure adding another human being to the mix is the best thing for the planet.

More than all of that, I'm so thrilled and complete with where my life is. I'm just grateful for right now.

TO THE CURIOUS ONES LIKE ME:

At this point in my life, with my 30th birthday fast approaching, I feel so, so lucky to have gone through everything I went through—the good and the bad. It's made me the person I am today. I can't imagine my life going any differently. I've learned so much.

I've learned how to be strong. How to not ever give up. How to not stop (even when maybe I should have stopped!). How to be good to people and care for people. How to just get up every day and get through it, no matter how things might be.

And most of all, and at the end of the day, I've learned that The Beatles were right.

All you need is love.

Of course, there's still a lot more learning for me to do. I want to learn more about the world, which means doing more traveling. I find myself growing as a person every time I travel and experience a new place I've never been, marvel at things I've never seen, meet interesting people and learn how they live.

Beyond that, I want to be a great wife—now that I've found an incredible man (after a couple of false starts), I want to make sure I take care of him as well as he takes care of me. Plus, I want to take care of my family, who struggled for so long. And I want to be a great leader for my team, and do the best work for my clients.

So I work on those things every day.

I admit, sometimes it all makes me a little tired. My life is really, really full. I've been going non-stop for about ten years. But when I get tired, I think—some people don't have an opportunity like I do to make a difference in the world.

And some people will never have that chance.

So I think about the people I've lost, and honestly, I want to do it for them. To keep working hard and living life full out to honor them and their legacies.

Mostly, it comes back to Brady. When I think about my stepbrother, who was curious but never got to learn where his curiosity would lead him, I remember to never take anything for granted and always live as big as I can for him. I still think about him a lot—about how funny and curious and full of life he was, and I laugh. I loved my time with him so much. I just wish there had been more of it. I wish he were here now, so I could help him follow his dreams, and share in his excitement when he discovered new things.

Sadly, he's not. But you are.

That's why I want to make sure that if anyone reading this book feels slighted and not understood—because they're different, because they're curious, because they don't fit into a box—they should never give up.

After all, look at me.

I have learned first hand that there is a place for everyone in the world. So always be who you are and don't ever feel like you have to change. Ignore what other people think you are, or think you should be, and be true to yourself. You'll find that there are people just like you in the world that are curious…you just have to keep pushing forward and finding your way.

I believe that the most curious people are the most unique people in the world. And yes, sometimes you might feel like the whole world is against you…I know I did. But somehow, I found the strength to keep going and to never give up.

My struggle made me want to see what was possible. To push the boundaries. To not let people define me.

To never conform. EVER.

I wouldn't be the same person if things had been easy for me. Those years feeling out of place, shopping with food stamps, drinking powdered milk and trick-or-treating in homemade Halloween costumes made me strong. They made me wise before my time. And I wouldn't have it any other way.

So my advice to you, wherever you are in life, is to take what you have and run with it. When you don't have any choice other than moving forward, that's just what you do. If you just keep going, you'll figure it out along the way.

You can have nothing and make something.

Yes, you will screw up. Yes, you will fail. Know that, and have the strength to start over again. That's the beauty. You have that choice.

So when it all feels like too much, when you're overwhelmed or depressed or just can't take it anymore, do what my mom told me to do.

Take a shower, shave your legs (if you're a girl!) and get going! There's no time to be sad, there's only time to be had.

Carpe Diem baby. Never, ever, ever give up.

Keep believing in yourself and your purpose—and be VERY SURE you are good to everyone you meet. Because you never know what battle someone is battling. So open your heart and let it guide you.

It will get you far.

That, my friend, is my hope for you. I hope more people live every day full out. None of this halfway BS.

Live the life you want. And love it.

Even the hard stuff.

Chapter II

GIVING THANKS

If the only prayer you ever say in your entire life is thank you, it will be enough.

—MEISTER ECKHART

M any books have a lot of pages of acknowledgements—and I think that's awesome. But there are so many people that have played such an integral part in my life and me becoming the person I am, I can't even begin to thank all of them.

So I'm giving all of you a BIG thank you here!

THANK YOU, THANK YOU, THANK YOU, THANK YOU!

You know who you are. :)

However, there are thirteen or so incredibly important people that need their own pages…so I'm going to give them those pages now.

Starting on the next page…

MOM & BOB

Thank you for never giving up on me and being patient and letting me figure it out. For always being my biggest fans no matter how many times I screwed up. Thank you for putting up with me when I was trying to balance my checkbook and for being okay with my persistence with everything!

And above all—thank you for giving me the greatest thing in the world: Love.

You are the most incredible parents a girl could ever ask for. My life is dedicated to you.

ALICIA & JESSICA

How awesome is it that my best friends are my sisters?
I love you both more than the world. More than words.
You're my rock (or, I guess I should say, my rocks!), my
light, and my inspiration every day. Without you, I don't
think I would have survived everything we went through.

Thank you for loving me just the way I am—and for
shining the light for me when I wasn't able to. For always
letting me sleep in your beds when I couldn't be with myself.

For letting me go completely crazy and loving me
anyway.

DAD

I'm so grateful for our short time together. Thank you for loving me unconditionally. Your time was cut short on this earth, but I'm proud that I come from you. I hear I have your smarts...and Uncle Mark said I have your sense of humor and sense of adventure, too!

I'll continue to make you proud.

Always and forever.

SHELDON

I was always so proud to tell people you were my big brother. You were such a protector over us girls. We all took a piece of you with us when we went out into this world. Your light shines so bright each and every day through all of us.

I'm even learning to love fast cars and motorcycles. I'm enjoying the ride for you.

Every day.

BRADY

You have the most tender place in my heart. The title of this book is for you. Because you and I—we were always curious—and always left behind by this hard world in so many ways. I loved you so much for being so much like me and understanding me. You were always challenging me and always teaching me.

I miss very much our late nights talking about life— still, to this day. I'll cherish those conversations forever.

I'm carrying you with me as I keep being curious about life. And I'll never leave you behind. You're here with me—always.

MASON

You will always be a curious one, too. And you're also the most intelligent person I know. I was always in awe over how you won every board game we ever played…and how you could read book after book effortlessly.

It was so inspiring.

I know times were tough for us, but I'm forever grateful for the person you are and the person you are destined to be.

Stay curious and never stop. You're as special as they come.

GRANDMA MYRT & GRANDPA BUD

You both are so important to me. It means so much that you never stopped loving me for who I *am*, no matter what I *did* or what mistakes I made. You're also the only people in my life that give me hope for this world—and for monogamy!

You taught me to never stop and never settle for less than I deserve. To always search for the kind of love I always dreamed about. Thank you for always being such a force in my life. I love you both endlessly.

GRANDMA FOYE
& GRANDPA FRED

Your lives ended way too soon, but I'm so thankful to be part of the Brown family.

You have created some of the most amazing children— and you both live through them each and every day.

Most importantly—thank you for my mom! She's an incredible human being and I know it's because she came from both of you.

Your love lives on and on.

THE BERLER FAMILY

Thank you for creating the most incredible human being I know—your son, Mark. He blows me away every day… and I'll be indebted to you all forever for giving me such a gift.

And to Allison and Matt—thank you for allowing me to be part of your lives. I'm dedicated to you.

I love you all so much.

OH, AND YOU, TOO! <WINK>

> You just have to believe in yourself...
> especially when others don't believe
> in you. Keep pounding on that door,
> because if you pound long enough,
> someone is going to open it.

–CHELSEA BERLER

I think it's also important to acknowledge the fact that I've learned a lot from some not-so-great people, too. In those moments, during those difficult, even painful encounters, I've probably grown more than I have at any other time in my life.

Sometimes, the greatest teaching comes from the non-believers.

So, for all of you who said I didn't have a chance…

For all of you who laughed at my ideas…

For all of you who judged the way I grew up…

For all of you who were (or are) not interested in my struggle and only care about my success…

This is for you.

I'm incredibly grateful for each of you.

If it weren't for you saying it couldn't be done...I wouldn't be where I am today. My interactions with you were the ones that kept me going, that kept me working harder and harder.

The ones that kept me pounding on that door.

So cheers to you. My hope for you is that you live the life you love—and that you start believing again in the "impossible."

Stay thirsty, my friends.

CONNECT WITH CHELSEA

ON THE WEB

- mostlychelsea.com
- solamaragency.com

SOCIAL MEDIA

- twitter.com/chelseaberler
- facebook.com/mostlychelsea
- pinterest.com/mostlychelsea
- instagram.com/mostlychelsea

FOR SPEAKING OPPORTUNITITES

- hello@thecuriousbook.com
- 800.780.8388

KEEP IN TOUCH WITH THE CURIOUS ONE

- thecuriousbook.com
- facebook.com/thecuriousbook